MW01054009

Paper Profits: How to Buy & Profit from Notes—A Beginner's Guide

Learn the nuts and bolts essentials of owning mortgage notes and why these assets consistently out-perform almost any other investment ever created.

JOSHUA N. ANDREWS

Copyright © **2017 by Joshua N. Andrews**

All rights reserved.

Published in **The United States of America**

ISBN-13: 978-1541296015

ISBN-10: 154129601X

No part of this book may be reproduced in any form unless written permission is granted from the author or publisher. No electronic reproductions, information storage, or retrieval systems may be used or applied to any part of this book without written permission.

This publication is designed to provide accurate and authoritative information in regard to the subject matter covered. It is sold with the understanding that the publisher is not engaged in rendering legal, accounting, or other professional services. If legal advice or other expert assistance is required, the services of a competent professional person should be sought.

DEDICATION

To my friend Bill McCafferty, who has done more than anyone to help me learn, grow and profit in this business.

CONTENTS

ABOUT THE AUTHOR

Joshua N. Andrews specializes in buying and selling mortgage notes with an emphasis on distressed assets. His passion is financial freedom through sensible investment choices. He believes in today's economy the real currency of life is time, not money.

In addition to debt instruments such as notes, Joshua has experience with single-family rental properties, small multifamily syndication, and stock-related assets. He is cofounder and CFO of Notable Investments, LLC. He has held the position of loan originator with two banks and is federally licensed through NMLS. He currently resides in Austin, Texas.

Joshua N. Andrews
Notable Capital Management, LLC
www.notablefund.com
josh@notablefund.com
Office: 512-572-6900

PREFACE

I believe everyone should strive to be financially independent. Achieving that, as I define it, means having a cash flow large enough to cover your living expenses—without having to drag yourself out of bed and into an office each morning to earn it. I have a favorite analogy that explains how I look at investing. In the days before agriculture, tribes would get up each morning to forage for food. Each day was the same. Wake up and gather the day's food. Then along came farming and agriculture. Now the tribe could work hard on the front end, planting food and tending crops, and then reap a large and more predictable harvest. Their existence became much more predictable, less tenuous. They could also store part of this harvest to reseed next year's fields, which meant their crop yield would grow over time. They could predict with relative certainty how much food they could expect to grow the following season. No longer was theirs a day-to-day existence. This changed everything. And it literally allowed people enough free time to break away from the cycle of merely *surviving*. It gave them more time to spend on worthwhile endeavors such as philosophy, art, music, medicine, and science. Ultimately, it allowed us to evolve.

Today, much of the world's population is stuck in a financial rut of day-to-day existence. Although we benefit from many technological advances, such as cars, computers, phones, advanced medicine, and so on, many of us are still stuck in this cycle of getting up each morning and going to work in order to bring home the proverbial "food" to pay our bills and feed our families.

We are, at some level, just financial hunter-gatherers. We need to find a more effective way to earn an income. A way that helps provide a continual supply of money that meets our needs so we can expand our interests and make our *lives* richer. This includes spending time with loved ones and family and having the time to contribute more to society. To me, this represents our next evolutionary step. Regardless of how much money you make, if you have to be physically present somewhere to earn it each day, it could all stop if you don't—or can't—show up.

Financial independence is certainly not easy to achieve. There's no real shortcut to riches. It takes time and a plan to become truly stable. It takes financial knowledge and personal grit, and it may require you to take a few well-calculated chances. The long-term rewards, however, are more than worth the struggle.

It all hinges on **acquiring assets that produce cash flow.** I can think of few things better to strive for.

INTRODUCTION

The desire to share the biggest financial discovery of my life motivated me to write this book. By all accounts, it's a secret hiding in plain sight. It's not a get-rich-quick scheme or a new hot stock tip. In fact, it's been around for hundreds and hundreds of years in many different forms.

I'm talking about promissory notes, mortgages, or, as they're more often known, notes. If you own a home, you are all too familiar with that monthly mortgage payment that goes to the bank. But have you ever wondered what the bank really does with those payments? There is a whole side of the mortgage industry that most people do not even know exists—let alone understand.

I worked for several years as a loan originator, approving mortgage loans for people, but it took me a long time to fully understand how they worked. Like most people, I thought banks made money simply from charging the highest interest they could get away with on their loans. This is not the case. This book will show you how much more profit there is in buying a promissory note than is commonly thought.

In this book, I share the fundamental information about mortgage notes you will need to understand what makes them great assets to buy—for small and large investors alike. I will show how you can start buying them with as little as $10,000 and generate wealth, security, and ultimately a safe retirement.

Like most individual investors, you probably do not know much about this topic yet. I will do my best to speak in plain language so that even if you've never heard about these debt instruments before, you will come away with a good understanding about how to evaluate, buy, and sell them yourself. You will undoubtedly have questions after reading this book. That's OK. Feel free to reach out to me.

It takes a lifetime in the mortgage market to completely understand its every nuance. You can make excellent profits with notes, however, using a basic understanding of how they function and where the opportunities are. My hope for this book is that it will help open your eyes to this unique investment opportunity. It can change your financial life—it has mine. We will take a bird's-eye view and cover the basics, answer some commonly asked questions, and briefly touch on more advanced ideas. I will share a few personal, specific deal examples as well. After you understand the fundamentals, you will be ready to analyze, buy, and profit from these little gold mines yourself!

If you are a seasoned note investor with a few deals under your belt, you will still pick up a good idea or two from this book. If you are a novice just learning the ropes, I recommend starting from the beginning and reading the book straight through in its entirety. This is about education, becoming financially literate, and having some fun along the way.

So let's get started!

CHAPTER ONE

THE ULTIMATE INVESTMENT VEHICLE

Wealth is the ability to fully experience life.
—Henry David Thoreau

Why Notes?

This chapter explains why notes are quite possibly the best investment ever created and how I came to discover this for myself. I will also cover some of the main reasons notes are ideal tools for generating long-term, repeatable returns and sustainable wealth.

For the better part of a decade, I have been searching for a way to create passive income. I'm not talking about multilevel marketing income, being self-employed, or having small-business income. I'm talking about real, honest-to-goodness income that would come in each month regardless of whether I worked or not. I looked at, explored, and invested in literally dozens of legitimate investment ideas. That's when I first began learning about commercial real estate. Multiunit buildings like apartment complexes are attractive to investors because they provide economies of scale and promise large-scale passive income. I have also purchased single-family rentals. I have purchased dividend stocks to try to generate income. I have owned a small business. After being actively involved in all of these attempts at generating passive income, however, I've decided that buying and holding notes are my favorite way of generating income over the long term.

How I Learned about Notes

I remember exactly when I first heard about the opportunity years ago. I was on the phone with a financial advisor, a wealthy man himself who had agreed to a thirty-minute phone call with me. The goal of the call was for him to counsel me, in a nutshell, on growing passive income. At the time, I was focused on building a portfolio of rental properties, and I had my mind set on buying a four-unit apartment building. I explained to the advisor that I had saved up a sizable down payment—sizable to me at least—and that I was actively looking around the country for the best market. In the course of our conversation, he casually mentioned I should look into "buying a few notes." I dismissed the idea and steered the conversation back to buying rental property. However, as we were about to hang up, he again said, "Take a look at buying a few notes. I can see you, retired, with several million dollars' worth of notes in your IRA."

That stuck with me.

Months later, I finally took the time to read up on notes and mortgages. I wanted to see if they made sense for my situation. After buying a few for myself and watching how they performed, I became hooked. I am still hooked today. Sometimes it's the small comments we initially dismiss that make the most difference in our lives.

Fast-forward to present day. Today I continue to invest my own money in notes, and I partner with other select individuals to help grow their passive income as well. I am fortunate to have a great network of friends and other acquaintances who have become investors in this business.

Why Notes Are a Superior Investment

Notes provide unique advantages to investors, but many of these are not initially understood by the layperson. But the concept of how they work is easy to grasp once you understand what a note is and how they generate profit.

Notes Are Ideal for Many Investors Because:

Real Safety and Control

Notes and mortgages are secured by property. The kinds discussed in this book are secured by single-family homes and are similar to the mortgage you may have on your own home. These loans provide a tangible level of security because they are secured by the collateral: *the property itself.* This means if the borrower stops paying and defaults, the lender—the investor who owns the note—will have legal recourse to sell the property in order to recover much or all of the money owed. This is different from other types of investment such as stocks, mutual funds, and more speculative ventures that may have no safety net or tangible way of recovering money if market conditions change. Notes provide safety for the investor, and that equates to peace of mind. As with any investment, I would be remiss to say there are not risks. There are. We will cover those later in this book and outline ways to mitigate and manage them.

You Decide the Rate of Return

When you own a note, people are essentially making their mortgage payments to *you* each month. When you purchase a note for yourself, enter a joint venture with another investor, or even join a note investment fund, you choose up front how much profit you make. This is different from other forms of investment like stocks, mutual funds, or even real estate—with those, you depend on the market or appreciation to increase your earnings, and that appreciation is largely or wholly outside your control.

Notes are different. With notes you know exactly, *down to the penny*, how much income they will generate for you each month. And they pay out consistently—for decades. This makes it easy to project your income and finances well into the future and to create a financial plan with great accuracy. Depending on the type of note, they can produce income of 8–12 percent interest each year, sometimes more.

Notes Are Discounted

Imagine a scenario where a borrower owes a mortgage of $50,000 at 6 percent interest, secured by a home. You can buy that note for $32,000 today, even though the borrower owes $50,000. So you bought the note for $32,000, but they owe you $50,000. That's a discount. If the borrower refinanced the home or decided to pay off the loan tomorrow, you would still receive $50,000, which is a profit of $18,000. If they don't pay off early—and most don't—then you can simply collect the income stream via the monthly payments each month.

Buying at a discount means you are buying ownership of the note for less than what the borrower currently owes. This locks in your profit, and it protects you from the possible event the borrower pays the loan off early. So in this example, even if the borrower paid off the loan tomorrow, you still come out very nicely! This, combined with choosing your own return and having your investment secured by real, tangible property, makes for a powerful, secure combination that's hard to beat.

Largely Passive Investment

In many cases, you can simply buy a note and watch the borrower's payments be deposited into your account each month. Depending on the type of note purchased (more on that later), there can be very little maintenance or management associated with owning notes. Most of your bookkeeping regarding the payments and balance are handled by your servicer or fund manager. There is no ongoing time commitment required from you. What's more, notes generate cash deposits, right into your account each month. This happens every time the borrower makes a mortgage payment—it goes to you. It is a truly wonderful thing.

Involved in Real Estate without the Hassles

When you own a note, you assume the position of lender, just like a bank. In this situation, you are not the *owner* of the property, the borrower is. The borrower owes you money, and that amount is recorded in the note and mortgage. The mortgage is secured by the home. This means you, as a note owner, have no obligations whatsoever for the property's upkeep. You don't need to worry about taxes, repairs, vacancies, zoning issues, homeowner association rules, or anything else. The borrower will never call you to come repair a leaky toilet or to complain about other repairs that are needed. That's his problem. Once properly set up, you—the note holder—simply collect a check each month. Mine are deposited via ACH, (direct deposit) so I don't even have to visit the bank.

In many cases, owning notes is easier than owning rental real estate. This is because there are a lot of significant moving parts to manage when you own real estate. If you own a rental property, you have repairs, vacancy, tenants, lawsuits, taxes, day-to-day management, and other time-consuming details to worry about. Not so with notes. With notes, you are also dealing with a different mind-set. You are dealing with an owner of a property, who has a homeowner mentality, not a renter mentality. Owners tend to take much better care of their properties, for starters.

There is no denying real estate can be a wonderful asset. And over time it can appreciate in value. However, for ease of use and predictable monthly cash flow, owning a note is hard to beat.

Note ownership is not tied to geographic location. You can buy notes nationwide, regardless of what your local investment or housing market is doing. Notes are also less susceptible to swings in the market or real-estate bubbles, although these do play a role in how much the property securing the note will ultimately be worth.

You have little, if any, direct correspondence with the borrowers. They don't call you if something is wrong or needs to be fixed. They fix it themselves, because it's *their* home. I cannot remember a single time a borrower has called me to complain about a leaky roof or other issue. The only reason I can think of a borrower might call would be simply to ask for another mortgage payment coupon for the month, so he knew where to send the money!

Ideal for Self-Directed IRAs

Notes can be purchased for a self-directed retirement account very easily. Your retirement account would be the legal owner of the note, and the borrower would send the monthly payment directly to that retirement account each month. Think about what this means for a tax-deferred or even tax-free account. If you have twenty years until you retire, for example, you could easily calculate how much cash will be in that account at the end of that term. This is compound interest at its simplest.

Imagine owning a note that pays you 10 percent interest annually. The borrower deposits the payments into your IRA each month, for ten or twenty years. No up years or down years, where you lose some then (hopefully) gain it back. Just steady, almost boring deposits. You can do the math. This is a reliable, safe, and better way to plan for retirement than investing in stocks and hoping the price goes up so you can sell off your portfolio at a profit and enjoy the good life.

Compound interest! Because your retirement account is receiving mortgage payments each month, once you have accumulated enough payments, you can go out and buy another note.

This makes it easy to compound wealth over the long term, over and over.

CHAPTER TWO

MORTGAGES AND NOTES DEFINED

A bank is a place where they lend you an umbrella in fair weather and ask for it back when it begins to rain.
—Robert Frost

What and Why

This chapter explains the basics of how mortgages and notes work. They are two separate documents that *together* legally secure a loan to a property. That property serves as collateral for the lender. I will also cover the differences between being a note owner and a landlord who owns property.

Mortgages are mentioned in English common law documents that date back as far as 1190. These documents illustrate the beginnings of the basic mortgage system as it still exists today. They describe how a creditor is protected in property-purchase agreements. Specifically, a mortgage started out as a conditional sale where the creditor held the title to a property until the debtor could sell that property in order to recover the money paid.

What does that really mean for us today? Essentially, a mortgage is just a loan secured by a property. Most people don't have the liquid capital required to purchase a house in cash, so a mortgage helps them purchase a home they would otherwise be unable to afford.

When a borrower approaches a lender to help him or her buy or refinance a property, that lender generates two legal documents: a mortgage and a note. These outline the terms of the loan arrangement and make it official, and they record the transaction in the public records, to protect the lender in case of default. Default scenarios happen when an individual takes out a loan and does not pay as agreed. This could happen for a variety of reasons and does not necessarily make the borrower a bad person or a deadbeat. Most people who buy homes are hardworking, honest individuals. We have all fallen on hard times at some point. The borrower may experience a financial hardship, job loss, income reduction, illness, or other unforeseen event that prevents payment as agreed. Lenders need a way to protect themselves against this, however, and recover their money in the event the borrower stops paying for any reason. This is why mortgages and notes exist as legal documents.

It is important to understand that a mortgage and a note are two separate documents.

The Mortgage

This may also be called a "Deed of Trust," depending on the state where it originates. This document secures a lien against the property title in favor of the lender. This secures the lender's interest in the collateral in the event of default. This means if the borrower stops paying the lender can legally foreclose, take ownership of the property, and sell it to recover the funds lent. Mortgage documents are recorded in public records and stay attached to a property until the loan has been paid in full, or satisfied.

The Promissory Note

This spells out the terms of the loan. Think of this as an IOU. It outlines exactly how the mortgage is supposed to be repaid. The note will specify, in detail, items such as the repayment schedule, rate of interest, due date, any prepayment penalties, and ultimately the date by which all funds need to be paid in full. In layman's terms, it is **a promise to pay** from the borrower. The note document may not show up on ordinary title searches.

When you hear investors talk about "buying a note," what they are really referring to is both of these documents.

Often beginning investors don't fully understand what they are buying when they purchase a note. You obviously don't own the property, so what exactly are you buying? **You are buying all legal rights to the note and mortgage, which are really just pieces of paper. It is the borrower's promise to pay, legally attached to the collateral—their property.** It is a publicly recorded and legally enforceable IOU, and it outlines terms and penalties for the borrower and legal remedies available to the lender in event of default.

Put a more optimistic way: you are buying the rights to an **income stream.**

Basic Note Owner Rights

- to receive payments from borrower as outlined in the note and mortgage.
- to sell or transfer ownership of the note to anyone, for any price.
- to enforce the provisions of the documents, which include acceleration of the sums due in the event of default. Remedies include foreclosure and/or selling the property.

Rights a Note Owner Does Not Have

- cannot physically enter or inspect the property.
- ownership of the property—that belongs to the borrower.
- cannot take any actions outside what is outlined in note and mortgage.
- Cannot change terms of the loan unless the borrower agrees in writing. This is called a loan modification.

This is different from what real-estate investors encounter. They are used to owning property. It's important to understand that in this position **you are not the property owner.** In many cases, from an investment standpoint, it's more beneficial to *not* be the property owner. This greatly reduces your liability and administrative burden. You don't need the headaches, midnight calls from tenants, and hassles.

Just like with any other investment vehicle, there are various niches in the market you can focus on. As an investor, you can buy notes on virtually any type of property—secured or unsecured. Some examples:

- residential (homes with one to four living units)
- commercial (apartment complexes, strip malls, hotels)
- mobile homes (single mobile homes or entire trailer parks)
- raw land
- automobiles
- defaulted credit card debt

Start with $10,000

You can buy a note starting with as little as $10,000. Because virtually anyone can get involved, there is tremendous opportunity for investors to begin earning excellent returns. You can enter the market using your savings or retirement money, through a self-directed IRA (see chapter 7).

My company focuses on purchasing notes attached to *single-family homes.* These are residential homes where the borrower and family live in the property as a primary residence. I buy these loans because the borrower usually has a vested interest in making the payments and paying on time. My line of thinking is that everyone has to live somewhere. My experience has shown that someone who owns their own home will do almost anything to make that payment, provided they have a job and have sufficient health to work and support the family. There are many types and flavors of note-buying opportunities, but this is the one I have come to prefer.

Basic Terms to Know

Performing

This is a note the borrower is paying on time, as agreed. Usually the payments are monthly, but they can be based on any time frame depending on the loan terms.

Non-performing

This is a note where the borrower has stopped making payments and has entered into default. Many times this was not the borrower's intention—it's often because they have fallen on hard times. They may have lost a job or are going through a divorce or have health issues. This simply means the note owner is not receiving payments as outlined in the note and mortgage. Many times this can be remedied through a loan modification or other remediating scenario.

Re-performing

This is a note that fell into a default situation where the borrower stopped paying for one reason or another; then, usually through a loan modification or some other form of agreement with the lender, the borrower started paying again. You will hear this term used when the borrower has made at least six to twelve months of on-time payments and is current.

Secured

This means the loan is secured by collateral, which protects the lender. The security or collateral is most often a home or property. This is the best type of note to own, in my opinion, because if something unfortunate happens and the borrower stops paying, the note owner can enforce the terms of the mortgage and sell the property to collect much if not all of the money owed.

Unsecured

This is a note with no collateral backing. The borrower still owes the money, but if they default the lender has no collateral to sell to recoup the money owed. This is a risky position to be in as a lender. I do not recommend ever buying unsecured loans, unless they are practically given to you or if you have a highly-specialized system in place for debt collection. There are large businesses that specialize in unsecured notes, such as credit card and consumer debt. These can be lucrative but are not recommended for the beginner or intermediate investor.

Unpaid Balance

This is also known as "UPB." It refers to the amount the borrower *currently owes* on a note. This does not include any arrears, missed payments, or late fees that may apply. This ties into yield and discount calculations, which are discussed in chapter 10.

Where Do Notes Come From?

There are three main avenues through which notes are created and enter the marketplace:

Banks

When money is loaned on a real-estate transaction, the lending bank creates a note and a mortgage, which can also be called a Deed of Trust (DOT) in some states. The act of creating a loan is called "origination," or "originating a loan." Banks originate the majority of home loans in the United States. Many of these loans are later sold to downstream investors, especially if they become troublesome for the bank. This typically happens in a default situation, where the borrower has discontinued making payments. There are many good deals to be had for a private investor interesting in acquiring notes handed off from a bank.

Individuals

A common lending method that involves just the seller and the buyer is called "seller financing." This type of lending can take many forms. The most common scenario is when Ma and Pa Jones want to sell a home they own. They would rather not worry about whether the buyer qualifies for bank financing, and are willing to act as the bank in this transaction. Ma and Pa Jones are the sellers, *and* they effectively lend money to the buyer to purchase that home. The buyer gives Ma and Pa a down payment then starts making payments to them each month, just like the buyer would to a bank. This can be a great benefit to all parties if structured properly. Ma and Pa sold their home the way they wanted, and the buyer got what he or she wanted—a home. It's a win-win. Seller financing provides value because it helps folks who may not be able to qualify for traditional bank financing. A note and mortgage are still generated to document the transaction.

Private Lending

This happens most often in the real-estate investment world. Private lending is often referred to as "hard money." People who provide private lending tend to prefer short loan terms, often one- or two-year terms, but they can be as short as six months. Private lenders have their own criteria for lending and prefer certain types of assets. These lenders are essentially investors or investment companies who have access to large amounts of capital and lend like a bank. Each time they lend, the money is secured by an asset, and it creates a debt for the borrower. Notes and mortgage documents are generated to document the transaction.

CHAPTER THREE

WHY INVEST IN NOTES?

Those who understand interest earn it; those who don't pay it.
—Anonymous

What and Why

This chapter explains the three main components of notes and what makes them powerful investments: yield, discounts, and the amortization schedule. I will also share an example or two from my own files.

The primary reason to buy a note is to make money and get paid each month. It's as simple as that. You will hear people talking about investing in notes to better humanity, help homeowners, and all sorts of nice and fluffy-sounding things. While it's true that we never want to take advantage of anyone and should be fair and ethical, the fact of the matter is that **you invest money to get a return.** That's the bottom line. If buying gummy bears were a wealth-building tool, I would be excited about that, too.

I sometimes question if the term "investor" is a very good description for the majority of people who buy notes—buying a note is simply more like being a small bank instead of investing.

How Do Banks Operate?

Banks lend money to get principal and interest returned in the form of periodic payments. They lend money on things that have collateral, which helps protect them from loss. Contrary to popular belief, banks do not lend for business ideas, stocks, or bonds. They only issue loans when the borrower has collateral. Collateral is an asset the bank can access to recover its money should the borrower default.

Other than applying for a credit card, when you visit a bank and ask for a loan, the first thing they will ask you is: *What collateral do you have to secure the loan?*

They do this to shift the risk to the borrower. In the event of default, the bank can take whatever property is needed to recover the money. This may sound harsh, but the bank is really just protecting itself. Truth be told, banks don't want to take back property or for collateral to be sold. They just want those interest payments coming in each month. That's how they make their money.

Note-buyers should have the exact same mentality. It is a hassle and it costs money to foreclose on a home to recover your investment. Unless your investment model is different, your main focus should be to have the borrower paying like clockwork every month. And then you can just forget about that loan and go out and buy another one!

Determining Profit

There are two profit "yardsticks" investors look at when determining if a note is worth further study or possible purchase. These are not all-inclusive considerations but are excellent starting points.

Yield

This is what most investors are focused on. **Yield is the interest rate**

your money is earning on a yearly basis, also known as "per annum." Think of this as a measure of how hard your money is working for you. A thing to keep in mind is that high yield does not mean high safety. Typically, the higher the yield, the riskier an investment is. I discuss calculating yield in detail in chapter 10.

Discount

This is when you buy a note for less than the face value owed by the borrower. Let's use an example. Say the borrower owes $32,552.66. You reach an agreement with the seller to purchase the note for $18,000. You now own the note. The borrower starts sending his monthly payments to *you* each month. You have spent $18,000, but the borrower owes you $32,552.66—plus interest. This is called "discounting" or "buying a discounted note."

Notes Are Discounted for Two Reasons:

1. There is always a small chance the borrowers could pay the loan off early. They *could* pay it all off, in full, tomorrow. To ensure that you profit in a scenario like this, you need to pay less than the amount the borrower owes when you buy the note.

2. In the majority of cases, you will receive your profit in small monthly payments over time. This happens when the borrower pays you each month. Remember that many residential mortgages are for ten-, twenty-, or even thirty-year terms. Because of the time value of money (TVM) and inflation, you should not pay full price for the note. More on this in chapter 5.

Amortization Schedule

This is where investors start to see the magic. **An amortization schedule is a complete repayment schedule for the loan.** It outlines *exactly* how much principal and interest will be paid in each payment, and when. An amortization schedule applies to all fully amortized loans—especially home loans. Amortization is how debt is paid off, outlined in a fixed repayment schedule in regular installments over a period of time. At the end of that time, or "term," the loan will have been repaid in full. There are also loans that are "non-amortizing," which means at the end of the loan term, there will still be a balance due. These include interest-only-type loans or balloon loans. For the purposes of our discussion, we do not need to cover these. I truly believe most people need to see an amortization schedule to really understand the power of what's going on here.

I promise I will do my best to avoid boring you with tables and charts, but stay with me here to learn how powerful an investment vehicle this truly is.

Look at the following amortization schedule. This is the initial loan information:

Compound Period: Monthly
Nominal Annual Rate: 7.000 %
CASH FLOW DATA

	Event	Date	Amount	Number	Period	End Date
1	Loan	1/25/2017	$ 35,552.66	1		
2	Payment	2/25/2017	$ 275.64	240	Monthly	**1/25/2037**

AMORTIZATION SCHEDULE - Normal Amortization

	Date	Payment	Interest	Principal	Balance
Loan	1/25/2017				$ 35,552.66
1	2/25/2017	$ 275.64	$ 207.39	$ 68.25	$ 35,484.41
2	3/25/2017	$ 275.64	$ 206.99	$ 68.65	$ 35,415.76
3	4/25/2017	$ 275.64	$ 206.59	$ 69.05	$ 35,346.71
4	5/25/2017	$ 275.64	$ 206.19	$ 69.45	$ 35,277.26
5	6/25/2017	$ 275.64	$ 205.78	$ 69.86	$ 35,207.40
6	7/25/2017	$ 275.64	$ 205.38	$ 70.26	$ 35,137.14
7	8/25/2017	$ 275.64	$ 204.97	$ 70.67	$ 35,066.47
8	9/25/2017	$ 275.64	$ 204.55	$ 71.09	$ 34,995.38
9	10/25/2017	$ 275.64	$ 204.14	$ 71.50	$ 34,923.88
10	11/25/2017	$ 275.64	$ 203.72	$ 71.92	$ 34,851.96
11	12/25/2017	$ 275.64	$ 203.30	$ 72.34	$ 34,779.62
2017 Totals		**$ 3,032.04**	**$ 2,259.00**	**$ 773.04**	

The table above is a summary of the loan data, along with a payment schedule for each year. This shows how each part of the payment is allocated, both principal and interest. It also shows the running loan balance, and how it gets paid down over time.

Fast forward 20 years (240 payments or 240 months, whichever you prefer to call it), and we see the final payment and balance when it reaches zero in year 2037. You will notice the borrower has paid a grand total of $66,153.60 on this loan.

240	**1/25/2037**	$ 275.64	$ 1.99	$ 273.65	0	
2037 Totals		$ 275.64	$ 1.99	$ 273.65		
Grand Totals		**$ 66,153.60**	**$ 30,600.94**	**$ 35,552.66**		

Looking at the amortization table, pretend you purchased and now own this note. It is owned by your self-directed IRA or tax-deferred retirement account. Each month, you receive a deposit of $275.64. To determine the amount of money it will contribute to your retirement account, refer to the Grand Total amount. It becomes easy to see if the loan is not paid off early, this borrower will pay you approximately $66,153.60 in total payments. This also does not take into account possible late charges or additional fees and penalties.

It Gets Even Better

What if I told you that, instead of lending the $35,552.66 to the borrower yourself, you could *buy* this note for $18,000, as in our previous discounting example? Now you own a note where the borrower owes you $35,552.66, but *you* only paid $18,000. As mentioned previously, this is called "discounting" or "buying a discounted note." It happens all the time, and discounted notes are quite easy to find.

Loan Amount	Rate	Term	Payment
$35,552.66	7%	240 month	$275.64

Our Purchase Price
$18,000

Using this example, there are three likely outcomes for profit:

1. **Borrower pays the loan in full tomorrow.** If the borrower decides to sell or refinance, you receive a check for the outstanding balance owed. In this case, it's $35,552.66. After deducting your purchase price of $18,000 you will *net* a profit of $17,552.66, before taxes.

2. **Borrower makes all payments on time, for the full twenty-year term.** In this scenario, you will recover both the initial loan amount plus all interest. In looking at the previous amortization schedule, you will see these amounts combined equal $66,153.60. After deducting your purchase price of $18,000, you will *net* a profit of $48,571.30.

3. **Borrower defaults and is unable or unwilling to continue making payments**. In this scenario, you have legal right to accelerate the loan, call it due, and begin foreclosure proceedings. After you complete the foreclosure and have obtained the legal title to the property, you can dispose of it or sell as you see fit to recover the money owed by the borrower. Lenders use this method as a last recourse, but it is a viable and oftentimes profitable strategy.

You may be thinking that there must be other scenarios or problems that could crop up. And you would be correct. There are. Most deal with bankruptcy or low-equity positions in the property. We will address those later, in chapter 8. For now, I want to impress upon you the main idea: **almost every scenario ends with the outcome in the lender's favor and a profit being made.** By taking advantage of proper education and by finding mentors or experts in the field, you create extremely good odds of making money.

Buy More, Faster

Let's take a moment to review what we've covered. In the example above, you invested $18,000, with no further effort needed on your part. If the borrower pays as agreed, you will be paid a total of $66,153.60 over a twenty-year period.

But What If You Could Compound Your Returns Faster?

Consider how fast money is being returned to you. In most cases, the lender is receiving small monthly payments from the borrower. These payments accumulate over time and can be reinvested to compound returns. Put another way, when you have several notes sending you payments each month, these payments can be saved up until you have a sufficient amount to purchase an entirely new note. Over time, your portfolio will provide the ability to purchase additional notes at an *accelerated rate*, without additional cash input from you. Remember that most notes will be earning a yield of 8–10 percent. It's an excellent way to compound money over time.

Use Debt to Pay Off Debt

As a note owner, you have wonderful magic up your sleeve. How would you like to have *someone else* pay off your debts for you? Even better, what if that someone paid you *extra* money for the privilege?

Here's How

Suppose you have a large outstanding student loan balance. This balance totals approximately $110,000. Without question, you owe this money. It will need to be paid back with interest over time.

Here's the idea. Instead of making payments on these student loans from your own paycheck, **what if you purchased a note and *it* paid the student loans for you?** Let's take a closer look and see how this plays out.

Refer to the following loan amortization schedule. Let's suppose you purchased a note similar to the one in the following table. It presumes that the borrower owes $40,000.

Compound Period: Monthly
Nominal Annual Rate: 6.000 %
CASH FLOW DATA

	Event	Date	Amount	Number	Period	End Date
1	Loan	1/25/2017	$ 40,000.00	1		
2	Payment	2/25/2017	$ 239.82	360	Monthly	**1/25/2047**

AMORTIZATION SCHEDULE - Normal Amortization

	Date	Payment	Interest	Principal	Balance
Loan	1/25/2017				$ 40,000.00
1	2/25/2017	$ 239.82	$ 200.00	$ 39.82	$ 39,960.18
2	3/25/2017	$ 239.82	$ 199.80	$ 40.02	$ 39,920.16
3	4/25/2017	$ 239.82	$ 199.60	$ 40.22	$ 39,879.94
4	5/25/2017	$ 239.82	$ 199.40	$ 40.42	$ 39,839.52
5	6/25/2017	$ 239.82	$ 199.20	$ 40.62	$ 39,798.90
6	7/25/2017	$ 239.82	$ 198.99	$ 40.83	$ 39,758.07
7	8/25/2017	$ 239.82	$ 198.79	$ 41.03	$ 39,717.04
8	9/25/2017	$ 239.82	$ 198.59	$ 41.23	$ 39,675.81
9	10/25/2017	$ 239.82	$ 198.38	$ 41.44	$ 39,634.37
10	11/25/2017	$ 239.82	$ 198.17	$ 41.65	$ 39,592.72
11	12/25/2017	$ 239.82	$ 197.96	$ 41.86	$ 39,550.86
2017 Totals		**$ 2,638.02**	**$ 2,188.88**	**$ 449.14**	
360	**1/25/2047**	**$ 239.82**	**$ 0.97**	**$ 238.85**	**0**
2047 Totals		**$ 239.82**	**$ 0.97**	**$ 238.85**	
Grand Totals		**$ 86,335.20**	**$ 46,335.20**	**$ 40,000.00**	

We can see that if the note pays as agreed over the term, the borrower will pay you a total of $86,335.28. This comprises both principal and interest on the loan.

 Here Is the Formula

Purchase two notes similar to this example, at a discount. Let's assume you purchase each for $20,000. This is a total cash outlay from you of $40,000. Every month, you will receive payments from the borrower. **Use these payments to pay your student loans. Yes, it is that easy.**

Deal Summary:

Amount of your student loans: $110,000

Cash outlay buying two (2) notes: $40,000

Total monthly income from notes: $479.64

Total income over term: $172,670.04

Here Is What You Accomplish

1. **Pay off $110,000 student loan balance.** You did this using only $40,000 of your own money.

2. **Made an *additional* $62,670.56.** You did this after paying your student loans in full. This additional money goes right in your pocket.

3. **Recovered your initial investment of $40,000**. In reality, the payments from two notes paid off your student loans, returned your initial $40,000 investment, *and* generated a profit of $22,670.56. (Profit is calculated by deducting the $40,000 from the $62,670.56.)

If there is an easier way to pay off debt, I'm not aware of it! This method can be used to pay off almost any type of debt. Think creatively and look for ways to use this to your advantage.

CHAPTER FOUR

COMPARING NOTES AND TRADITIONAL INVESTMENTS

Money doesn't always bring happiness. People with ten million dollars are no happier than people with nine million dollars.
—Hobart Brown

What and Why

In this chapter, I will compare note investing with other traditional options. I will preface this chapter by saying that any of the following investments can be good and profitable. Large amounts of money and wealth have been created in each.

In this instance, however, I am comparing them to what I know about purchasing note investments and how they differ.

How Notes Compare to Other Investments

Stocks

This is a very passive form of investment, and it's also one of the most volatile. With stocks you have very little control over the return. You do nothing other than perform as much research as possible and pick those that you anticipate may go up in value, split, or otherwise increase. In this scenario, the inventor has no real control over the company management or direction, including the choices its board makes. Because of this, the investor is basically "along for the ride." Also, to make money at some point, the investor will need to sell the stocks. He will need to buy low, let the stock rise in value or "appreciate," and at some point sell them for more money than he purchased them for in order to make money. Investors can also buy dividend-producing stocks, which pay out small amounts simply as a "thank you" for owning them. I purchased some of these in my early days of investing and can testify that although they do produce a very small cash flow, it is *so* small you'd be hard pressed to live on it as income—even with a *very large* amount of money invested. Another thing to understand about stocks is that the value is determined by what the market *thinks* the company is worth. Put another way, a stock is not collateralized with tangible property via a lien. A stock value is only based on past or anticipated company earnings. If the company fails or becomes insolvent, you have no recourse to recover your money. In many cases, it is simply gone.

Notes vs. Stocks

Unlike owning stock, owning a note gives you immediate monthly cash flow. Once you have a few notes in your portfolio, this monthly amount will likely be large enough for you to start paying bills with, or reinvesting the money. You also have complete control over each investment with notes, and the ability to retain the investment without selling while you reap a continual yield. It is also easier to compound money over time with notes. This is because the note owner receives payments from the borrower on a monthly basis (there's cash flow again). This money can be reinvested on a regular basis to compound returns. That is especially true if a note is purchased inside a self-directed IRA. (More details on that topic in chapter 7.) One last thing that makes notes far superior to stocks, in my opinion, is the fact that a note is secured by real, tangible property. This provides a safety net for the investor should payments from the borrower discontinue. This alone makes the investment much more secure.

Mutual Funds

These funds are a collection of stocks, bonds, and other paper securities in a portfolio, typically managed by a mutual fund manager. The manager can be a single person or a group of people. The manager makes the decision on what items to acquire and when to sell them. This is essentially a large "bucket" of paper assets chosen by the manager. There are fees charged to investors by the fund manager for being part of the fund and relying on the manager's expertise at creating a profitable blend of assets for the fund. Quite often the manager is paid based on the amount of volume or trading he manages, *not on performance.* In real life, this can mean that even if the manager picks the wrong assets and loses investors' money, he is still paid handsomely. This can create a conflict of interest or lead to situations where the investor is at a significant disadvantage. Investor portfolios in mutual funds can increase, decrease, or lose value altogether.

Mutual funds are not unlike stocks, with the exception that **someone else is making the decisions for you and charging you a fee regardless of the outcome.** Investors give up all control over performance and basic choices about what companies to invest in. While mutual fund managers are undoubtedly smart, the odds are not in the investors' favor long term. Although many managers *do* have their clients' best interests at heart, it's important to remember **they will be paid regardless of whether their investors make money.** This is not a favorable scenario for anyone other than the fund manager.

Notes vs. Mutual Funds

Notes provide a wonderful alternative to mutual funds. When buying notes, the investor still may choose to allow someone else to manage the assets, but the investor will still be involved in buying decisions. This can happen via partnerships, joint ventures, or participating in a note fund. Another key distinction already mentioned is the fact that notes are secured by tangible assets (the property). Investors in notes also receive an income stream each month, and they are not required to sell the note to in order to realize a return. Investors can of course sell almost any note for a lump sum of cash, should they so desire. Note investors are also completely immune to the fluctuations of the stock market, its ups and downs based on public perception of the global economy. The value of a note is based on a single piece of property, its performance, equity, and other tangible, easily measurable factors.

Bonds

Bonds are considered securities. We can think these as large notes or "IOUs." Bonds are typically issued by state municipalities, corporations and the federal government. Think of a bond as a loan. Except in this case it's not a loan to an individual, it's you loaning money to a large government or institution. These are considered safe, and as such they have very low yields. For example, the US Treasury bond, or "T-Bond," is a fixed-interest US government debt with a maturity of more than ten years. As of publication, owning a T-Bond gives an investor an annual yield of 2.77 percent. This is less than 3 percent interest per annum.

Once inflation is factored into this investment, an investor earning a 3 percent return on his or her money is losing value each year. Regardless of personal belief, many governments, including the US government, are very close to insolvency. This makes owning bonds even less attractive and less secure. Other nongovernmental bonds offer higher yields, but compared to a note investment, the returns are still low, and they do not provide the liquidity a note does. Nonetheless, bonds are still better than letting money sit in a bank savings account and earning less than 1 percent interest. Owning a bond is similar to owning a note in the respect that each requires very little effort to maintain once purchased.

Notes vs. Bonds

Bonds are fairly safe, but they provide little in the way of yield for the investor. The yield has been and continues to be too low to stay ahead of inflation. Buying a note is the best of *both* worlds. It provides an investment secured by property (the home), along with yields in the 8–12 percent range per annum. This puts investors ahead of inflation and grows their account over time. In addition, when notes are purchased within a self-directed IRA, the *entire amount* earned could be tax free, or at least tax deferred.

Tax Liens

This is a unique type of investment I see many people chasing. **A tax lien is placed on a property's title when the owner fails to pay annual property taxes.** This lien takes priority over all others, including a first mortgage lien. A tax lien is also called a "super lien" because of its status over all other liens. There is a principal amount attached to the lien, which is the amount of tax owed by the owner. There is also a high rate of interest attached to the outstanding principal. The property owner can redeem the tax lien by paying it in full at any time during the redemption period. This period can be anywhere from six to twenty-four months and varies by state.

Tax Lien Basics

1. A lien is created when a property owner fails to pay property taxes. After a predetermined period of time of nonpayment, a lien will be placed on the title of the property.

2. If the owner still fails to pay, the lien is sold on the open market to investors. The state or municipality is paid the tax money *from this sale.* This results in the state being paid in full and the buyer/investor taking ownership of the tax lien.

3. The buyer/investor now owns a superior lien on the property. The buyer is nearly guaranteed to recoup their principal investment plus interest. After purchase, there is something called the "redemption

period," where the property owner can redeem the tax lien from the investor by paying the amount owed. When this happens, the lien is extinguished and the buyer/investor makes a return on his or her money from the interest accrued.

4. Once the redemption period expires, if the property owner has not paid the amount due, the buyer/investor can foreclose, take ownership of the property via the deed and sell the property. Any junior mortgages on the home would receive any leftover funds from the property sale *after* the tax deed amount was satisfied. In other words, the amount owed to the tax deed is paid first, then any first or second mortgage balances would be paid from whatever funds were left over from the sale.

Many investors purchase tax liens with the hope of repossessing a property for pennies on the dollar. This does happen—but only on rare occasions. Usually what happens is the investor buys a tax lien and then waits for it to be paid by the property owner. In this instance, the investor receives a return of both principal and interest from their investment in one lump sum.

The downside for investors looking to generate cash flow is that they essentially have no income while waiting during the redemption period. Remember, this period can be as long as twenty-four months. During this period, you are **not receiving payments**. As such, you have no cash flow from the investment. While it's safe and therefore one of the better ways to invest, it is difficult to use tax liens as a vehicle for consistent monthly cash flow. You would need large sums of money—possibly millions of dollars—to provide monthly income consistent enough to live on. This is because of the redemption period and the payoff timing being infrequent.

Notes vs. Tax Liens

Tax liens address the safety and security component of investing considerations, but leave out the cash flow aspect. It's hard to pay your bills, take a trip, or retire from the income generated buying tax liens unless you are investing huge sums of money. As previously mentioned, buying a note provides the **instant cash-flow** component. Also keep in mind that a note will generally generate interest payments for *decades*, while a tax lien is an investment with a much shorter duration. There is also much less competition to buy notes, as many investors are not savvy about how they work or don't understand the dynamics of what makes them an ideal opportunity.

However, tax liens are still a viable strategy for investment, provided the investor keeps the lack of cash flow in mind.

Rental Real Estate

More wealth has been created in real estate than in virtually any other type of investment. That being said, there are drawbacks to owning property. You own a physical structure, and that comes with responsibilities and *liabilities*. Some of these concerns include: taxes, tenants, maintenance, repairs, property managers, and HOAs. The list goes on. You may also have a mortgage payment on the property each month. Many investors find it prudent to buy local real estate, in order to keep a close eye on it and/or to manage their properties themselves. This can be difficult when your local market is red hot—there may be no deals that make sense for you as an individual investor. It is also smart to have good cash reserves set aside for unforeseen circumstances or needed emergency repairs. Items like insurance, capital improvements, and vacancies can quickly eat up any monthly profit or cash flow you generate.

Real estate does have an upside. It tends to appreciate over time, and there are some excellent tax deductions available to property owners. When purchased correctly, it generates a good cash flow. It is certainly a viable investment vehicle.

Notes vs. Rental Real Estate

While it is true there is a learning curve to mastering investing with notes, it is a relatively easy and passive way to invest. Note-owners don't worry about repairs to the home, for example—the borrowers pay for them because it's *their* home. The borrowers pay the property taxes, because it's *their* home. Note-owners don't need a property manager. Note servicers provide a simple online portal through which you can check on your portfolio. You can do this on the weekend or when visiting family—from any computer. Another advantage to buying notes is the fact they can be purchased anywhere, nationwide. This means there is opportunity for you regardless of what your local real estate market may be doing. **Buying both notes and real estate together provides the best of both worlds: real estate for appreciation and tax deductions, notes for consistent and hassle-free cash flow.**

The Drawbacks of Note Ownership

After all my raving on the benefits of owning notes, seeing this section may come as a surprise to you. Nothing is perfect. To be fair, there are aspects of note ownership I wish were different. I believe these to be minor items, but they deserve mention.

Lack of Tax Savings

Current tax code allows for a large amount of deductions and write-offs for depreciation on real estate, especially rental properties. Not so with notes. Note income is taxed as *interest income.* This means your business can take the necessary write-offs, just like any other business, but you will never reach a scenario where you write off 100 percent of interest income. However, if you lose money with a note, you can deduct the amount as a loss, which does provide tax savings. It is important to understand that you are only taxed on the *interest portion* of the borrower's payment, which is your profit. The principal portion is not profit. It is called "principal payback" and treated as a return of your original amount invested. The best way to create tax savings with notes is to purchase them from inside your self-directed IRA. That is the ultimate tax savings plan. We have a special chapter dedicated to just this topic, chapter 7.

Notes Do Not Appreciate in Value

Unlike real estate, notes do not appreciate over time. While real estate *can* appreciate, by how much and when is outside your control. Notes, in fact, do the opposite. The value of the note stays almost static, and will go down very slowly over time as the borrower pays down the loan. Not a bad thing really, because you are collecting payments every month and putting that money in your pocket. However, it is important to point out that the value of the investment does go down as the loan is paid down. This is because any potential buyers for the note will be interested in the income stream the note produces.

The remaining amount of payments and the payment amount are some of the metrics buyers are looking at.

Notes Get Paid Off Eventually

Every now and then, a note you own will suddenly be paid in full. This is a sad day for you, as the income stream is suddenly gone forever. It's not all bad, however, because you will likely have made tens of thousands of dollars collecting those monthly payments before this happens. Hopefully you reinvested that money buying *more* notes. The types of notes we have been discussing carry terms of ten, twenty, or even thirty years, so we are talking about decades before the payments discontinue. That is, unless the borrower pays off the loan by refinancing or selling the property.

In either of those two cases, you will receive a large lump sum cash payment.

Three Main Considerations

When comparing investment options, the criterion I use is straightforward. I seek investment that protects the principal amount invested and that will generate regular and consistent cash flow. It's that simple. There are other considerations that come into play, but the general thought process is as follows:

1. **Safety.** Protecting the money invested.

2. **Return.** Realizing a return on the amount invested. It needs to pay back all principal, with additional profit high enough to beat inflation and gain wealth over time.

3. **Cash Flow.** Consistent and predictable cash flow. This refers to a stream of income that does not deplete principal, but rather increases over time. In a scenario like this, you can live off the interest your investments generate, without ever touching the principal invested.

The Rule of 72

An interesting calculation you may find useful is "the Rule of 72." It was developed as a guide for determining how fast your money will *double* in any investment. According to Investopedia.com, "The rule of 72 is a shortcut to estimate the number of years required to double your money at a given annual rate of return. The rule states that you divide the rate, expressed as a percentage, into 72."

Years required to double investment = 72 ÷ compound annual interest rate.

For example, a compound annual return of 8 percent is plugged into this equation—as 8, not 0.08—giving a result of nine years. The calculation is 72 divided by 8 = 9. This is a quick little equation that will help you understand how long it will take to double your money.

You can also reverse this equation. Let's assume you want to double your money in five years. What interest rate do you need to be earning? To figure this out, just divide five into seventy-two. An interest rate of about 14.4 percent would double your money in that amount of time.

A great online calculator for this can be found at:
http://www.moneychimp.com/features/rule72.htm

CHAPTER FIVE

INFLATION AND THE TIME VALUE OF MONEY

By a continuing process of inflation, governments can confiscate, secretly and unobserved, an important part of the wealth of their citizens. By this method they not only confiscate, but they confiscate arbitrarily; and, while the process impoverishes many, it actually enriches some.

There is no subtler, no surer means of overturning the existing basis of society than to debauch the currency. The process engages all the hidden forces of economic law on the side of destruction, and does it in a manner which not one man in a million is able to diagnose.
—John Maynard Keynes

What and Why

This chapter explains the effect inflation has on savings and living expenses over time.

I will also briefly talk about the time value of money concept (TVM). After reading this chapter, you will see why it is *vitally* important to invest money instead of just saving it.

According to Investopedia.com, here is the definition of time value of money.

"The idea that money available at the present time is worth more than the same amount in the future, due to its potential earning capacity. This core principle of finance holds that, provided money can earn interest, any amount of money is worth *more* the sooner it is received."

It's important to understand what this means for investors—or anyone who saves money for the long term. Money today is better than money tomorrow for one simple reason: it can earn interest as time passes. The entire banking industry is founded on and works with this idea. The basic premise we need to understand is that a dollar today is not the same as a dollar tomorrow.

This is because:

1. Money in the hand today can **earn interest.** This grows the amount of principal over time.

2. Paper money becomes **less valuable with time**. This is primarily due to inflation.

How Inflation Affects Investments and Savings

This is a very in-depth topic that I will cover only briefly here. I mention it to impress upon you the importance of investing with an eye toward *earning a return on your money instead of just saving it.* Here is the basic concept. **Inflation is the gradual increase of prices for goods and services. Put another way, it can be described as a decline in the purchasing power of money.** You may notice that things seem to cost more each year. Everything from gas to groceries keeps increasing in cost, by approximately 3–5 percent each year. For an eye-opening experience, do some research and look back just a few decades at prices for common household goods. Or, ask your parents or grandparents how much they paid for their first house or car when they were growing up. I think you will be shocked at just how much prices have increased compared to just a few decades ago. And the prices of things continue to increase. Why is this?

Contrary to popular belief, it is not "normal" for the cost of goods and services to increase. In fact, they should go *down* over time. During our short lifetimes, we have been conditioned to think these increases are normal simply because it's all we have ever known.

Take a moment and think about it. Logic says that costs for goods and services should remain the same or even go down as time goes on. This is because most goods and services become more efficient to produce as production methods improve, technology advances, and scalability increases.

This is in fact true. When a commodity is first introduced into the marketplace, the cost to consumers is quite high. Early adopters pay a premium, which helps fund research and production. Later in the production cycle, initial research costs have been recovered and production has been streamlined. So in effect, production costs less over time.

According to InflationData.com, the average inflation rate from 1989 to 2015 was 3–5 percent. **This means that the cost of goods and services is increasing 3–5 percent each and every year.** Now, it's true the exact inflation rate can be argued and a number of complex factors are involved. Many of these factors are beyond the scope of this book. This is why I mention a 3–5 percent range; it's simply based on the data available.

What This Means for Us in the Real World

- **It costs 3–5 percent *more* each year to buy the same items.** This means $10,000 today will not purchase the same amount of goods and services five years from now.

- **Money saved is worth 3–5 percent less each year.** Or, put another way, it buys 3–5 percent fewer goods and services each year. Here is an example: If you save $100,000 today and it earns no interest, it will only be able to purchase $70,000 worth of goods and services ten years from now. That is assuming a steady 3 percent inflation rate. In short, you will have *lost* $30,000 simply due to inflation.

- **Our purchasing power is going *down* or being eroded 3–5 percent every year.** This is how savers become losers. You can save over a lifetime and still be barely able to make ends meet at retirement, simply because of the slow creep of inflation.

Due to the points just mentioned, it is imperative the money you save is invested and earns a rate of return, preferably above 5 percent per year. It's easy to see that **with inflation you literally cannot save enough to provide for a safe and secure retirement.** Unless you have a massive windfall equal to winning the lottery, saving alone is not enough. Unfortunately, many people do not understand this fundamental principle or what is really happening to the value of money over time.

This is why owning notes can be so powerful. Notes provide the ability to earn above-average returns on a consistent basis. These returns are well above current inflation rates, which serve to protect your money and to keep it growing. This is the *key* to a safe and secure retirement. Notes are also wonderful for the fact that you know *exactly* what you will be earning each month. Notes are not a moving target, nor do they involve speculation.

What Causes Inflation?

Contrary to popular belief, inflation is not a naturally occurring phenomenon. Inflation is caused by world governments printing gargantuan amounts of paper, or "fiat," money and injecting it into the economy. As "more money chases fewer goods," the price of the available goods is bid up. Simply increasing the money supply increases prices. There are a number of complex economic factors in play behind this, but in essence printing of fiat money is what causes prices to rise each year. You will hear all manner of excuses and reasons why inflation occurs, but **it all boils down to governments printing too much money and diluting the money supply.** More supply means each dollar is worth less each year. And because each dollar is worth less, you need more dollars to make purchases for the same goods and services every year.

For more study on this topic I recommend reading *Ludwig von Mises on Money and Inflation*. It is great reading for the serious student of investing and finance. Another great resource is www.inflationdata.com. I have no affiliation with the website, but it provides good statistical information.

In the long run, inflation comes to an end with the breakdown of the currency.
—Ludwig von Mises

Our Generation Is Different

Past generations could live frugally, saving until the day of retirement and then retire on savings alone. Oftentimes the money saved would also be enough to ensure a great standard of living. Companies offered pensions to people who worked there for twenty or thirty years, which is an excellent retirement solution. For most people today, this is no longer a viable option. Inflation, longer life expectancy, and many other factors make simply trying to *save* for one's retirement a loser's game. **Saving is good, but it needs to be coupled with sound investments that earn a return.** In short, the money needs to be *earning* money and growing.

The key idea I hope you take away from this chapter is to **keep your money earning interest.** If you are just saving, you are losing. You cannot save enough to have a great retirement. Common sense shows that. But you can invest enough in cash-producing assets to enjoy the standard of living and lifestyle you and your loved ones deserve.

Compound Interest Is Your Friend

A great way for investors to protect themselves from inflation is to compound their earnings. Due to current tax code, this works well inside a self-directed IRA. Depending on how it's structured, you can defer taxes or even compound them, tax-free. This is a huge advantage, since taxes eat up much of the "growth" you could otherwise reinvest. Let's take a look at a couple scenarios.

Let's assume you have $50,000 in your IRA now. You have roughly twenty years until retirement, and can continue contributing $6,000 each year. If you could take advantage of compounding, either with notes or another investment vehicle generating 10 percent interest, what would that amount look like at retirement?

Compounding your investment returns annually at 10% interest and adding $6,000 in yearly contributions (currently the max contribution as of this writing), **in 20 years you will have $680,024.99.**

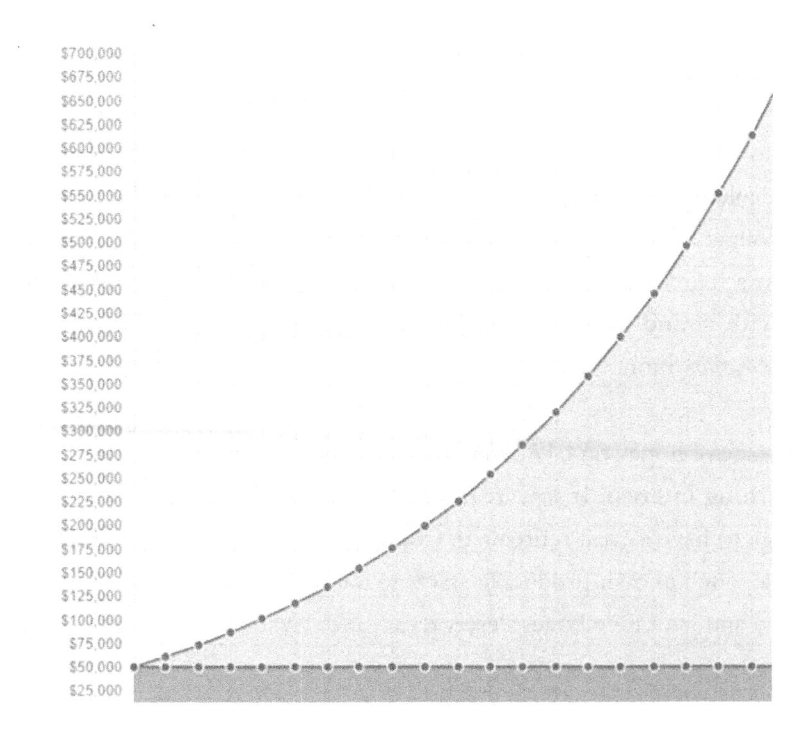

Not bad! Let's say you are a little closer to retirement—you're fifteen years away. You have $250,000 in an IRA. Here's what that looks like.

Compounding your investment returns annually at 10% interest and adding $6,000 in yearly contributions **in fifteen years, you will have $1,234,946.93.**

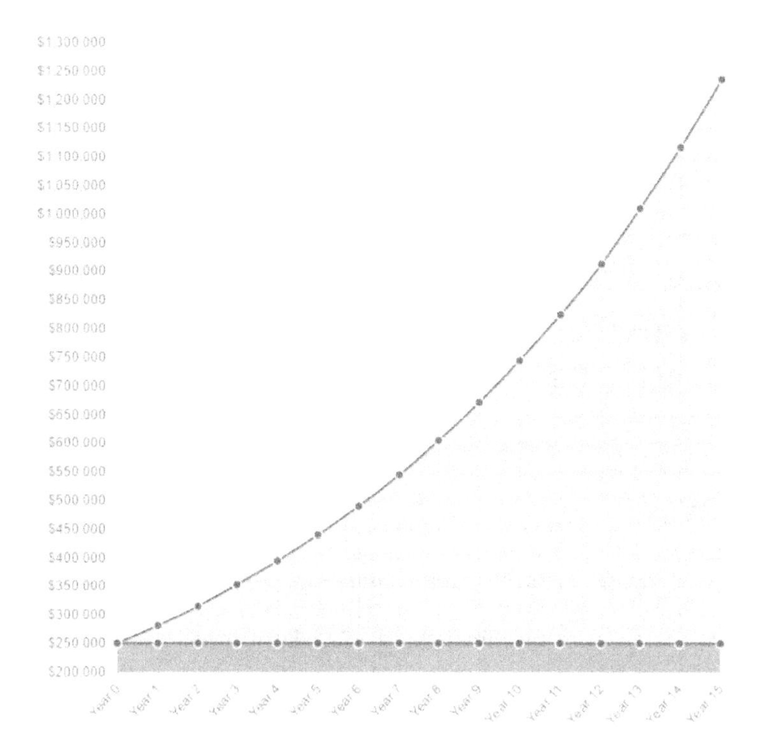

As you can see, there is real power in compounding earnings over time. This can create fortunes and change the retirement landscape for those who plan wisely.

CHAPTER SIX

PERFORMING PROPER DUE DILLIGANCE

And when our lives are defined by our choices, the all-important question becomes, how do we make good ones?
—Gary Keller and Jay Papasan, *The ONE Thing*

What and Why

This chapter covers methods used to investigate and evaluate a potential note purchase. In the note business, this is also known as "due diligence," sometimes referred to simply as "DD."

In the real world, asset preservation is key. It is important to protect your money by making the soundest investment decisions possible. Like any investment, a note needs to be carefully analyzed before purchase. Not every note is a winner, and yes, you can lose money investing in notes. This typically happens, however, when you fail to take the time to fully research the note you are buying. Taking the time to educate yourself on the asset is important because there are various nuances to each opportunity to be aware of *before* you buy.

Merriam-Webster defines due diligence as:

1. The care that a reasonable person exercises to avoid harm to other persons or their property.

2. Research and analysis of a company or organization done in preparation for a business transaction (as a corporate merger or *purchase of securities*).

In layman's terms, due diligence refers to the steps we take to investigate an investment and to verify whether it meets our buying criteria. Depending on the type of investment being considered, there can be multiple steps to this process.

Investment risk is managed by performing due diligence before purchasing any note as an asset. If you are a beginner, I recommend getting the assistance of a seasoned note investor who has been involved in many transactions. This is ideal, because a mentor can look over your shoulder to provide guidance and constructive feedback and often point out things you may not see. This guidance is invaluable, and it's the way I learned to invest.

An important item to consider when deciding if a note is worth buying has to do with **equity.** I am talking about equity in the property being used as collateral. Typically, this will be a single-family home (or a building of one to four units). **Equity is the additional amount the property is worth over and above the loan(s), liens, or encumbrances on it.** Or, stated another way in the context of real estate: the difference between the current market value of the property and the amount the owner still owes on the mortgage. It is the amount that the owner would receive after selling a property and paying off all mortgages.

Here's an Example

A home is worth $100,000.
The borrower owes a first lien of $50,000. This is a note and mortgage secured by the home. There are no other liens on the property.

In this scenario, the equity, or *remaining value above the loan(s)* is $50,000. So we say there is $50,000 of "equity" in the property. This $50,000 is your cushion as a lender or note owner. It helps provide that sleep-well-at-night feeling. It is no coincidence that banks look for equity when you apply for a home loan. Typically, they are looking for 15–20 percent equity in the property (often your down payment). This means they will only lend up to 80–85 percent of what the home is worth. This 15–20 percent equity protects them in the event of default, ensuring they will have enough left over to cover any attorney's fees, real-estate agent fees, or associated items should they need to foreclose, sell the home, and recover their money.

Here's Another

A home is worth $100,000.
The borrower owes a first lien $50,000. This is a note and mortgage secured by the home. The borrower also owes a *second* lien of $25,000, which is also a note and mortgage against the home.

In this scenario, the property has two mortgages. Combined, the borrower owes $75,000. If the home is worth $100,000, the remaining value "left over" after both mortgages are paid is $25,000. This means there is $25,000 worth of equity in the property. In this example, we are not accounting for real-estate agent fees or commissions should the home be sold, or any attorney's fees for a foreclosure, etc. This is simply to illustrate the equity concept. Again, this $25,000 is protection or "cushion" for the lender or note owner.

General Rule of Equity

- **More Equity = More Safety for the Lender**
- **Less Equity = Less Safety for the Lender**

Loan-to-Value and Combined-Loan-to-Value

Loan-to-Value (LTV)

This is a calculation used to evaluate risk on secured assets, typically a home mortgage. You calculate it by dividing the mortgage amount by the property's value.

Example: John's home is worth $300,000. He has a mortgage secured by the home for $200,000. Simply divide the mortgage amount by the property value. In this case the answer is 66.66 percent. So the LTV is 66.66 percent. This means John has 33.34 percent, or $100,000, of equity in his home. This $100,000 is protecting the mortgage owner in the event of default.

Combined-Loan-to-Value (CLTV)

This is just like the LTV calculation, but it accounts for *all* secured loans on the property. Many homes have one, two, or even three secured mortgages on them. In these cases, it is important to know how much real equity is protecting the lender(s).

Example: Steve's home is worth $150,000. He has a first mortgage secured by the home for $100,000. He also has a second mortgage secured by the home for $40,000. He owes $140,000 total. Again, simply divide the combined mortgage amounts by the property value. In this case, the answer is 93.33 percent. So the CLTV is 93.33 percent. This means John has 6.67 percent, or $10,000, of equity in his home. This $10,000 is all that's protecting the mortgage owner—bank or note owner—in event of default.

Obviously, this is a much thinner margin of protection than the previous example and probably not enough to cover a real estate agent's commission should the home be sold.

Managing Risk with LTV and CLTV

You can see how understanding basic metrics of mortgage finance, like equity and LTV, are important to assist with risk evaluation. Of course this is only part of the process, and there are other factors to consider. As strange as it may sound, I regularly purchase notes that have little or even zero equity. Why? Because these can be extremely profitable. I am able to pay a fraction of the cost of the face value of the note because I understand that there is risk involved. I also do a great deal of research on the borrower, the property, the details of the borrower's initial loan transaction, and his or her apparent ability—or inability—to continue paying the mortgage. I manage risk by performing extensive due diligence and by paying less for higher-risk assets.

How to Think like a Note-Buyer

Most buyers are primarily interested in the income stream, or cash flow, a note produces. There are essentially two questions every buyer should ask:

1. What is the likelihood the borrower will continue making payments?
2. What is my risk if the borrower defaults?

Performing due diligence helps answer those questions and puts into perspective how valuable this income stream may be, while defining what you may stand to lose. Remember, **note buying is really the business of buying an income stream.**

First in Time, First in Right

As mentioned previously, a property can have multiple mortgages against it. We briefly talked about first liens, second liens, and third liens. A good question you may be asking yourself is, in the event of a default situation, who gets paid? Do *all* the mortgages get paid? Like many things in life, the answer is—it depends.

Here is how you find out. There is a rule called "first in time, first in right." It establishes the priorities of liens recorded against a property. This rule states *who gets paid and in what order* in the event of a foreclosure or liquidation. In layman's terms, this means whichever lien was recorded first on property title is in first position to be paid in the event of a default or sale.

The priority of a lien matters in the event of a foreclosure. The holder of the lien with the highest priority is paid first from the proceeds of the sale. Only after that party is made whole does the holder of the next-highest-priority lien receive any money from the sale. This continues down the list of liens until they are all paid—or until no more money is left. If there isn't enough money for all of the lienholders to be paid, the holders of the lower, or "subordinate," liens simply don't get *any money at all.* Liens that were recorded before others have priority—this is what denotes a first lien, second lien, etc.

Here's an Example to Illustrate

John and Mary are buying a home. An appraisal report shows it is worth $300,000. They do their research, work with a realtor, and close the sale. They pay $300,000. In addition to the first mortgage, they also take out a second mortgage to help finance their home.

Purchase price: $300,000
Down payment: $60,000
First mortgage amount: $200,000
Second mortgage amount: $40,000

Remember, this home is worth $300,000 at the time of purchase. Several years later their home goes up in value, to $350,000. They see no harm in using their equity, so they take out another $50,000 loan to pay for a nice backyard pool. Now they have a *third mortgage* on the home. Five years later, however, the housing market drops, and their home is now worth only

$240,000. Mary loses her job and they proceed to fall behind on their mortgage payments. In this scenario, *any* of the lenders can legally foreclose, so long as their loan is in default. However, only the first two mortgages will be paid from a sale of the house itself. There is simply not enough equity, or "value," from the sale to pay the third mortgage. This is why the priority of a lien matters. This is obviously an extreme example, but it shows how both borrowers and lenders can easily get themselves into trouble if a property is over-leveraged.

This is not to say you should only buy first-position notes. I frequently buy second-position notes; when purchased with adequate due diligence, they are extremely profitable and excellent assets to own. The key thing to understand is what you are buying and at what price. Many notes exist that would appear to a novice or outsider to be junk but are actually excellent deals.

Always Do Your Homework—Trust, but Verify

Below are several of the many of the items I review when considering a note purchase. The process will vary depending on the type of loan being purchased and how much money is at stake, but this will provide you with a starting point for your due diligence.

Collateral Documents

I ask the note seller for copies of the note and mortgage. I read *the entire document* to confirm the payment, rate, borrower information, and origination date and to familiarize myself with the language stating the lender's rights in the event of default. I also get a copy of all "assignments and allonges." These are the running records of all past and current owners of the note. It is like a chain of title, showing who has owned the note in the past, who owns it currently, and when it was transferred. The note seller will provide these items for your review.

FMV Estimate

I use online resources to get a fair market value (FMV) of the property. I am looking for a general idea of value, not an exact price. I use www.realtor.com, and www.zillow.com, for example. Keep in mind these are rough estimates and should not be used as absolute numbers—they can vary wildly from any actual sale price. I compare three sources and use the *lowest* value from the three as the value for my calculations. The company RealtyTrac, www.realtytrac.com, also offers a paid service (at the time of publication, $49 per month). It shows you in-depth information about property history, location, current ownership, crime rates, and many other very useful data points. If you are a serious investor this subscription is worth the money.

Google Street View

This may sound elementary, but it's amazing what you can find out about a property using this tool. I take a quick look at any address I'm considering to ensure I am not wasting time researching a dump—or a vacant lot. It also gives an instant visual of the outside condition of the home, the neighborhood, and the area in general. This is all useful to know.

Borrower Payment History

If the note is performing, I ask the seller for a payment history. This should show the last six to twelve months of payments made by the borrower. I want proof the payments are being made on time, which can be obtained by getting copies of the cashed checks. This can sometimes be difficult, as people do not like to release this type of information. A better way to get proof is from the servicer. This is the third party servicing the loan. They can provide documented payment history, which I find to be more reliable anyway. I like servicers because they are neutral to the pending transaction. Although accounting errors can be made, it is rare and a servicer has nothing to gain by hiding the truth from you, whereas the seller does.

Servicers

A servicer is a company that collects payments from the borrower on your behalf. They are your "face" to the borrower. A good servicer will be licensed, be bonded, and follow proper guidelines in order to keep you

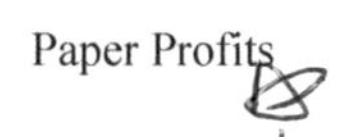

compliant and out of legal messes. As a note owner, you must adhere to a whole barrage of lending laws. These include Dodd-Frank and the Fair Debt Collection Practices Act (FDCPA), but there is a *myriad* of others. A servicer helps you comply with these. Servicers send out required disclosures and documentation to the borrower on your behalf. They also send out monthly statements, including end of year 1098 mortgage interest statements for the IRS. They collect the payment from the borrower each month and deposit the funds into *your* checking account. Having a good servicer on your team is key to staying compliant with lending and servicing guidelines, which can change quickly and frequently.

Servicers I use are:

FCI Lender Services www.TrustFCI.com

Madison Management Services, LLC www.MadisonManagement.net

Borrower Credit Reports

Depending on the type of note, it can be useful to review the borrower's credit report. Second-lien investors in particular will need to have a copy of the borrower's credit for review, which is sometimes provided by the seller. Reviewing credit can give you an excellent understanding of the borrower's financial situation. This includes the amount of loans outstanding, how borrowers utilize debt, and if they have a habit of paying late or defaulting on their obligations. I do not place all that much importance on credit scores, however, as some of my best notes have been associated with borrowers who had low credit or FICO scores. I tend to avoid notes with borrowers who have a FICO below 500, though, as this can be an indicator of a habitual credit abuser and nonpayer. It is important to remember that this is sensitive personal borrower information and should be treated as such and not shared with others. Being cavalier with this can cost you dearly.

PACER Records

The acronym stands for "Public Access to Court Electronic Records." Believe it or not, nearly all court records are available to the public. I use PACER primarily to check for bankruptcy filings. Knowing if a debtor is in bankruptcy is important because it can tell you about the financial wherewithal of your borrower, which in turn triggers a search for past filings. You will need to set up an account through PACER to access this type of information. To access filings, you will need the borrower's first and last name, along with the last four digits of his or her social security number. These two pieces of information should pull up any filings in the last ten years. A note that is in bankruptcy usually does not harm the position or validity of you as the lender—it only slows down a foreclosure or collection action. It does not wipe the debt away or make it uncollectible, except in the rarest cases, depending on the state. Avoid purchasing a note where the owner has completed or is currently in a chapter 13 bankruptcy, as there are small details that can get you into trouble.

Order Title Reports

If the review of all the pieces above went well, I also pull a title report on the property. The note's seller will do their best to tell you what a great deal you're getting, but ***it's your job to verify everything***. I recommend ordering a title report called an "O&E report." This stands for "ownership and encumbrances." I check all liens, mortgages, judgments, and the tax status on the property from the last property purchase to the current date. I also review a copy of the vesting deed. An O&E title search is ideal for foreclosure auctions, pretax auctions, short sales, tax sales, tax certificate purchases, non-performing note transactions, by-owner transactions, and refinances and to check for a clear title. You will receive a title report on all outstanding mortgages, liens, and judgments recorded against the property and its current owner(s). I recommend using www.ProTitleUSA.com. This report can cost anywhere from $49 to $200, depending on the county.

Once I receive the title report (typically takes twenty-four to forty-eight hours), I review it closely. Don't take shortcuts with this step. Title reports are complex, and it's safe to say you will see a variety of information you may not understand. Items to look at closely include the current vested owners and how many and what type of liens are on the property. This includes what position your note may be in (first, second, third, etc.). There can be multiple mortgages and other liens, such as HOA liens, tax liens, city municipal liens, and so on. All of these are important to know about before making an offer to the seller. I will not cover these in depth, as they could fill a book by themselves. I strongly suggest you have someone familiar with title review look over your first few transactions. He or she may catch something important you might have missed.

Order a BPO

If I have gotten this far with my due diligence and the note still looks like a winner, I may order a broker price opinion (BPO), especially for first liens. It is similar to an appraisal. However, since neither the note's holder nor you actually own the home, by law there's no way to enter the premises to perform a full appraisal. So the next best thing is a BPO. They will pull up the sales history of the home, tell you about the neighborhood and geographic area, and give you basic information on the sale-worthiness of the property. If you have looked at the property value online and the BPO comes in lower, err on the side of caution and go with the lower BPO number. Take some time to review the BPO once you receive it. Pay close attention to the comparable properties used, and to any comments made by the agent. These can tell you a great deal about the asset's quality. A BPO costs around $99 or $150, depending on the state and area. I recommend using www.lres.com.

Tip: Much of the due diligence process is free—it only requires your time. However, title reports and BPOs cost money. Before you spend that money unnecessarily, come to a verbal agreement with the note seller on a sales price. Simply come to an agreement with the seller on a price of $X, *subject to* completion of the remainder of your due diligence, which is review of title and BPO. You may adjust your offer price if you find something on either of those documents that is not appealing. This will help protect you from spending money researching every asset that comes your way. Once you have a verbal agreement with the seller, it's usually safe to spend the money and order these items.

Keep in mind these are general starting points to get you used to performing the basic level of due diligence; as you become more advanced, you'll learn about additional research options available. Items like TLO reports, credit reports, skip traces, and other means of data verification all play a part in helping you determine a note's value.

The short list I've provided is a good general starting place for beginners. It's a brief overview of what is necessary to help you make an informed decision about a note. Depending on the type of asset, different steps may be required. For example, if you are buying a first-position note, you will want to check the property taxes and hope they are current. If you are buying second-position liens, you will want to have a copy of the credit report and make sure the first lien is being paid and is current. So just be aware that this list is general in nature.

You will notice this is a long chapter. There is good reason for this. **The key to successful note investing—and ultimately profit—is to be informed about what you are buying.** This requires knowing the fundamentals. If you have a full-time job, a family, and other responsibilities on your plate, consider partnering with someone on your first note purchase. There are many ways to do this successfully. One of them is to participate in a note fund.

Note Funds

These are legal structures that pool money from different investors in order to purchase notes. Investors participate by buying shares of the fund, which is typically structured as ownership shares in an LLC. By setting it up this way, investors participate in the profits as note owners. Profits can be a combination of equity and cash flow. Most common is a preferred rate of return, which is usually 8 to 10 percent interest per year, which the investors earn on their invested money.

This can be a great way for qualified people to earn an excellent rate of return while remaining completely passive. Passive investors can also use retirement or self-directed IRA money to participate in a note fund to compound their returns tax deferred or tax-free. More on this in chapter 7.

CHAPTER SEVEN

HOW TO PURCHASE NOTES INSIDE A SELF-DIRECTED IRA

The only preparation for tomorrow is the right use of today.
—Anonymous

For this chapter, I have asked Mr. Quincy Long to contribute his expertise regarding self-directed IRAs. Mr. Long is CEO and Founder of Quest IRA, Inc., a company with multiple offices to serve self-directed IRA customers nationwide. I am grateful for his expert contribution to this book.

H. Quincy Long, Certified IRA Services.
Professional (CISP), Attorney, President, and Founder of **Quest IRA, Inc.**
17171 Park Row, Suite 100. Houston, Texas 77084
Phone: 281-492-3434
Fax: 281-646-9701
Toll-Free: 800-320-5950
Email: Quincy.Long@QuestIRA.com

What and Why

This chapter talks about the basics of self-directed IRAs, including the advantages these vehicles offer and how to use one for investment purposes. We will also address common questions regarding how to safely purchase notes inside your self-directed IRA.

If you have a retirement account of some kind, possibly with a current or past employer, you may be familiar with a range of typical investment offerings. Your account probably offers a limited assortment of things to invest in, including items like mutual funds, stocks, and bonds. The general process is for you to pick a few "you feel good about" and then let the market do the rest.

While there is some value in this, you can typically do much better for yourself without being an investing genius. Because you work hard to save for retirement, it seems prudent to invest those savings into things you know and understand. After all, why work hard and save money if you are not reasonably sure it will grow and be there during retirement?

What if you could invest in things you knew, felt comfortable with, and understood fully? With a self-directed IRA, you can.

What Is a Self-Directed IRA?

The self-directed IRA is not an official classification. It is merely an IRA where the owner (in this case, you) makes all the decisions about what to invest in and how to structure those investments. Investments can range in size and scope. You can purchase real estate, multifamily buildings, raw land, notes, tax liens, oil and gas, and more. There are prohibited items you cannot purchase, however, including things like collectibles, antiques, and life insurance.

Can You Switch a Current IRA to a Self-Directed IRA?

The answer is probably yes. There are seven different types of plans that can become self-directed. These are:

- Traditional IRA
- Roth IRA
- SEP IRA
- SIMPLE IRA
- Individual or Solo 401(k)
- Health Savings Account (HSA)
- Coverdell Education Savings Account (CESA)

What Are the Advantages of Self-Directed IRAs?

These have many advantages over regular retirement accounts. A self-directed account allows you to have more options and flexibility than other types of IRAs.

Tax-Favored Treatment

As with all IRAs, 401(k)s, HSAs, and CESAs, self-directed accounts offer tax-favored treatment of contributions and gains. Gains are almost always free from taxation while they remain in the account (except for business income not previously taxed and debt-financed income within the account). Qualified distributions from Roth IRAs, Roth 401(k)s, HSAs, and CESAs are tax-free.

Control Over Your Retirement

Perhaps the most significant advantage of self-directed accounts over other IRAs is that they allow you to take control of your retirement funds so you can invest in ways you believe are most profitable or worthwhile. Instead of leaving your retirement funds exclusively in the hands of large companies listed on the stock exchange, where you have no control over their actions, you can choose to invest in companies and ventures that ensure you know where your dollars are going and how they are invested.

You Can Invest in What You Know

One of the best ways to reduce risk within your retirement portfolio is to invest in what you know and understand. If you are knowledgeable about investing in real estate or in promissory notes and mortgages, it seems rational to have at least part of your retirement funds invested in these types of assets.

Are Funds in a Self-Directed Account Still Tax Exempt?

Yes. There is no legal distinction between a "self-directed IRA" and the more typical brokerage-style IRAs that allow you to invest in stocks, bonds, and mutual funds. **The only difference is what the account agreement allows as investments.** All IRAs are governed by Internal Revenue Code (IRC) Sections 408 and 408A (for Roth IRAs). These place certain restrictions on investment activities through the prohibited transaction rules of IRC Section 4975.When buying an asset like a note or real estate, *the IRA itself* purchases the asset. In other words, the IRA is considered an entity that holds the title to the asset directly. The representative of your IRA is the self-directed *provider*.

What Is a Provider?

Companies called "providers" help facilitate self-directed IRA accounts for consumers. The provider's role is to supply proper documentation and paperwork to both the self-directed IRA account holder and the IRS. This needs to happen on an annual basis.

Think of a provider like a bank or stock-trading company. They help facilitate the transactions within your self-directed IRA account but cannot give you investment advice. They are examined annually and are required to have the appropriate bonding and insurance.

What Does a Provider Do?

A provider helps your self-directed IRA remain compliant with IRS regulations by providing the IRS with documentation about your account on an annual basis and keeps you abreast of changing IRA laws. This would be difficult to do on your own, though not impossible.

Provider services include:

- Providing education (but not advice) to clients and their advisors.
- Assisting clients in establishing self-directed IRAs and other self-directed accounts.
- Assisting clients with transferring funds from existing IRAs or former employers' plans to self-directed IRAs.
- Providing clients with the forms needed to open an account, transfer funds into an account, buy or sell assets within an account, and take distributions from the account.
- Obtaining from the clients (or other sources) the fair market value of the IRAs as of the end of each year and reporting this information to the clients and the IRS on IRS Form 5498.
- Reporting any distributions to the clients and the IRS on IRS Form 1099-R.
- Ensuring that investments made by clients in their IRAs are titled correctly in the name of their IRAs and not in their names individually. For example, [Self-Directed IRA Provider Name] FBO Joshua Andrews IRA #1234521.

What Do Providers *Not* Provide?

Self-directed IRA providers will *not* provide the following advice or services:

- tax advice
- legal advice
- investment advice
- review investment selections
- create or sponsor investments
- perform due diligence or guarantee any investment

Instead, providers rely on clear, written instructions provided by the client (you) to direct the account's activities. This is made abundantly clear in the documents used to open an IRA as well as the documents that relate to the purchase and sale of the investments, so be sure to understand your responsibilities. Self-directed IRA providers do *not* do the due diligence for you on potential investments, and they disclaim any responsibility for determining the suitability of any particular investment for an IRA.

How Do I Purchase Notes Inside My Self-Directed IRA?

The process is straightforward. You make an offer to the note seller, just like any other transaction. Once you have an agreement on price, you complete a purchase agreement. The note will be owned by your self-directed IRA, not by you personally. As an example, if I purchased a note, ownership of the note would be held like this: **"Quest IRA, Inc.—For Benefit of Joshua N. Andrews IRA #1234521."**

The IRA provider holds the title to the note asset, *for benefit of your IRA*. In this manner your account remains protected and compliant with IRS guidelines. In short, if you were to put the assets into your name personally, they would lose their tax-advantaged status.

When purchasing a note, you'll have to complete a few forms, which will be given to you by the provider. They are happy to walk you through the process. Then you simply instruct them to wire funds from your IRA to the note seller. That's it.

Now your IRA owns a note. The process can take a few more days than a normal note purchase, due to the paperwork involved. Most sellers will understand this.

Are There Any Special Concerns?

Purchasing a note, or even a pool of notes, is essentially the same whether being done inside an IRA or with your personal funds, except for the extra paperwork required by your IRA provider and how the assets are titled. You must do your due diligence for IRA note purchases as for any other note purchase—providers do *not* perform this service. Here are a few additional things to keep in mind:

How You Hold the Title to Assets

Notes are held directly in your self-directed IRA. Payments are collected from the borrower by your note servicer, as discussed previously. The payments are then deposited directly into your self-directed IRA. The payments never touch your hands personally. You can check and manage the status of the account online, much like you would a normal bank account.

Fair Market Valuations

Each year, your self-directed IRA provider is required to report the fair market value of the assets owned by your IRA. This is done on IRS Form 5498. Depending on the type of account, the value reported may have tax consequences, such as affecting the amount of your required minimum distribution (RMD). Even in the case of a Roth IRA, which requires no distributions, the value of your notes must be reported. The fair market value of your notes may be more or less than what you paid for them.

Generally, notes have a presumed value of the principal balance and any interest due at the end of each year, unless you provide evidence supporting a different value. Your self-directed IRA provider will send forms requesting the fair market value each year. The requirements for valuing assets come from the IRS, not from your self-directed IRA provider.

Unrelated Business Taxable Income (UBTI)

Although unrelated business taxable income (UBTI) will normally not affect the ownership of notes within your self-directed IRA, it is worth mentioning briefly. Most of the time, income and gains made within an IRA are not taxed until they are withdrawn, and with some types of accounts (like a Roth IRA) are never taxed at all. However, if your IRA owns a business, either directly or indirectly through a nontaxed entity such as an LLC, then it must pay taxes on its business income. Similar rules apply if the IRA owns debt-financed property either directly or indirectly. If your IRA receives business income or income from debt-financed property, you must arrange to have IRS Form 990-T prepared for your IRA. IRAs are taxed as trusts, and the tax rates go to the highest marginal tax rates with as little as $12,400 (in 2016) of unrelated business income. If the activity would be taxed as business income outside the IRA (for example, if you are a note flipper), or if there is debt incurred for the purchase, then this tax may apply. This does not necessarily mean you should not conduct this activity within an IRA, but you do have to understand and comply with the tax filing and payment requirements. If your IRA owes tax, the IRA must pay the tax from its own funds. There is no effect on your individual income tax return.

Where Can I Get More Information or Help Setting Up an Account?

Setting up an account is easy. It requires a little paperwork, which your provider will be happy to help you complete. There are many providers—some good, some not so good. One of the premier providers of self-directed IRAs and other plans is Quest IRA, Inc. Quest IRA has offices in Houston, Dallas, and Austin, Texas. They have very knowledgeable and friendly staff, and the owner, H. Quincy Long, is a Texas attorney and an active investor.

Visit their website at www.QuestIRA.com, where you can find a lot of great information on self-directed IRAs, as well as their schedule of events. You may also call them at 281-492-3434 or 855-FUN-IRAS (855-386-4727).

CHAPTER EIGHT

HOW FORCLOSURE AND BANKRUPTCY AFFECT YOUR INVESTMENT

There is no class of people in the world who have such good memories as creditors.
—P.T. Barnum

What and Why

This chapter explains the general concept and process behind foreclosure—or the taking back of property in order to recover your money in the event of a borrower's default. It will also cover bankruptcy basics and how they affect secured lienholders.

Let's talk about the elephant in the room. You may be wondering what happens if the borrower stops paying and defaults? **What is foreclosure, and what happens to my investment?**

According to www.investopedia.com the definition of foreclosure is:

"A situation in which a homeowner is unable to make full principal and interest payments on his/her mortgage, which allows the lender to seize the property, evict the homeowner and sell the home, as stipulated in the mortgage contract. One month after the homeowner misses a mortgage payment, he/she is in default and will be notified by the lender. Three to six months after the homeowner misses a mortgage payment, assuming the mortgage is still delinquent and the homeowner has not made up the missed payments within a specified grace period, the lender will begin to foreclose. The farther behind the borrower falls, the more difficult it becomes to catch up, since lenders add fees for payments that are 10 to 15 days late."

Each state has its own set of laws relating to foreclosure. The best way to become educated is to review the state laws before you buy a note for a property in any given state. **You do not need to know all the state laws by heart.** They do change, and it's a lot to keep in your head.

Here are resources you can refer to on state foreclosure laws. Keep in mind there are various nuances to each state's rules. Therefore, do a little study to understand what the rules are before pursuing an investment in a certain state. The company RealtyTrac has great resources on this.

State Foreclosure Laws:

http://www.realtytrac.com/real-estate-guides/foreclosure-laws

What Causes Foreclosure?

Despite popular belief, most people do not just wake up one day and decide to stop paying their mortgage. People often fall on hard times. Most people are not deadbeats, they just have a life event that causes them to fall behind.

In reality, only four things really cause people to go into foreclosure:

1. death
2. divorce
3. job loss
4. medical problems

As you can see, these things could happen to anyone. So I typically give folks the benefit of the doubt until they prove otherwise. This is a good rule of thumb for many things in life as well!

Types of Foreclosure

Judicial

This type of foreclosure goes through the courts and requires an attorney to handle most of the documentation and legwork. He or she he will typically do all the work and just send you the bill. Judicial foreclosure can be somewhat expensive, and it is time-consuming. Legal costs range anywhere from $3,000 to $7,000, depending on the circumstances. It is safe to assume a judicial foreclosure will take twelve to fourteen months in some states, sometimes longer. Each state has its own timelines that dictate how long a foreclosure takes and what steps need to be taken. Again, this is best handled by an attorney.

Non-judicial

This is the most convenient type of foreclosure—if there is such a thing. It is also the most cost effective. Most investors prefer this type, although I prefer never to foreclose *if at all possible.* Non-judicial foreclosures do not go through the courts but rather rely on language spelled out in the deed of trust, which allows the lender to begin foreclosure proceedings after certain default milestones have been hit and disclosures have been sent to the borrower. Depending on the state and circumstances it can take three to twelve months to complete. Costs range anywhere from $2,500 to $5,000. I recommend hiring an attorney, a debt collection specialist, or even a servicer to help you perform this type of foreclosure. Doing so protects you, and it also gives you one less thing to worry about. Another thing to keep in mind are the costs. Remember, it costs money to pursue a delinquent loan. The borrower will be paying for all these expenses from the sale of the home in the future. So while you may be putting up money initially to cover the expense, **the borrower or the home itself will be paying foreclosure costs in the end.**

What Happens after Foreclosure?

At the end of a successful foreclosure, you are given the deed to the property. **At that moment, you become the property owner.** The note you owned is now extinguished (no longer exists). As the owner, you have a variety of options:

1. Sell the property.
2. Rent the property.
3. Evict current occupants (if any).
4. Live in the property yourself.
5. Create a seller-financed note and receive income stream.

What I can say regarding foreclosure is that it's usually smart to hire a professional to buffer you from many of the day-to-day headaches the proceeding entails. This professional is usually your attorney.

If you are using a servicer, they can refer you to a foreclosure attorney whose experience matches your situation.

How Often Does Foreclosure Happen?

According to the Mortgage Bankers Association, "1 out of every 200 homes will be foreclosed on." While this sounds like a lot, consider that most individual investors will never own anywhere close to two hundred notes. I've experienced foreclosures from time to time, but they are not as common as you may think. You may own ten or twenty notes before someone falls so far behind on payments that your only option is to foreclose on the property. Even then it's not the end of the world by any stretch, because you have the property as collateral to recover most—hopefully all—of your money. Also, to be perfectly clear, yes you can lose money in a foreclosure but that happens rarely if you choose your note carefully before investing. With proper planning, education, and a good guide who has "been there before" you can lessen your risk on much of this and come out a winner 95 percent of the time. Those are pretty good odds for any investment, especially one secured by real property.

If you own thirty notes and twenty-eight are sending you regular payments each month but two go into foreclosure, is this really a disaster? You are diversified, so it won't make any real difference to your income. All your eggs won't be in one basket. This is one reason I am a big fan of buying multiple small notes instead of just one or two large ones. More on this idea in chapter 9.

What about Bankruptcy?

A common fear of many novice investors is that a borrowers bankruptcy will wipe out their note investment. Is this fear validated in real life? The answer *most of the time* is no. I say most of the time, because in rare instances a court order can been issued to make a note null, or invalid.

The two most common types of consumer bankruptcy are outlined below, so you can learn the basics about them. I will preface this by saying this is a broad overview of bankruptcy and is not meant to be comprehensive. I recommend studying more on your own to learn the finer details, as there are many.

My Borrower Filed for Bankruptcy—Now What?

Suppose you are notified that your borrower has filed for bankruptcy. By law, all lenders the debtor owes funds to must be notified of a bankruptcy action. What does this mean for you? It depends largely on the type of bankruptcy and your legal status as a lender. The most common consumer bankruptcies are Chapter 7 and Chapter 13.

Chapter 7

This type of bankruptcy is oftentimes referred to as a "liquidation" plan. In a Chapter 7, the bankruptcy trustee cancels or forgives most—or sometimes all—of the borrower's debts. The trustee may also sell any assets the borrower has to repay creditors. The entire process usually takes five to seven months to complete. When completed successfully, it is referred to as "discharged." This is, in essence, a fresh start for the borrower.

If for some reason a Chapter 7 is not completed successfully, it is referred to as "dismissed." Being dismissed basically treats the bankruptcy proceeding like it never happened, therefore the borrower still owes all his/her debts. A dismissal can happen for a number of reasons, some of which have to do with the borrower not being able or willing to comply with the trustee requirements.

In a successfully discharged Chapter 7 bankruptcy, many creditors lose their claims. This means the borrower is no longer personally liable for the debts, and the lender can no longer pursue or contact the borrower for payment. This happens frequently with *unsecured debt.*

Unsecured debt includes things like credit cards, consumer loans, cellphone and cable bills, and other accounts that are not attached to collateral via a note. Items that *are* secured by a note, such as houses, property, and even car loans, are not forgiven. With these, the borrower has the choice to do one of the following:

- Voluntarily surrender the items back to the lender.
- Reaffirm the debt and continue making payments.

What Happens to a House in Chapter 7 Bankruptcy?

In Chapter 7, borrowers do not automatically lose the home. They can choose to retain the home and continue making mortgage payments. They can also sign an agreement called a "reaffirmation agreement." This is essentially the borrower recommitting to the terms of the loan and promising to pay it. Since a note and mortgage are secured and attached to the property, it is not usually wiped away or made uncollectible in Chapter 7 filings.

However, there is some nuance to this. **When a Chapter 7 is discharged, the borrower no longer owes the money personally for the note and mortgage. The property owes the money.** This may sound a little strange, but the borrower has been forgiven of the *personal liability* for most of his debts. This includes a note and mortgage. That means you cannot pursue a judgment or sue the borrower personally for this debt—but *his home still owes the debt* outlined by the note and mortgage. With this protection in place, the noteholder still retains all rights to foreclose and sell the property if the note goes into default. So while this may seem a little strange, it is actually a great thing for a note holder.

Why do I say this is a great thing? Well, let's think about it. After successfully completing a Chapter 7, the borrower is free of the crippling consumer debt that was draining his bank account each month.

With these gone, he will have more money to pay his mortgage. My experience has been that most people will choose to retain their home both during and after bankruptcy.

If they don't, you can simply exercise your right as a lender and foreclose, then dispose of the home to recover your money. I think you will find completing a foreclosure is a rare occurrence, and in most cases a headache, but not a huge cause for concern.

For further information on bankruptcy:

http://www.uscourts.gov/services-forms/bankruptcy/bankruptcy-basics
http://www.nolo.com/legal-encyclopedia/bankruptcy

Chapter 13

A Chapter 13 bankruptcy is also called a "wage-earner's plan." It enables individuals with regular income to pay outstanding debts over time. With the help of a court-appointed trustee, debtors propose a repayment plan to creditors. This is a payment schedule that makes installment payments to creditors over a three-to-five-year period. The debtor retains most or all of his property, but agrees to pay back a portion of his outstanding debts over the agreed-upon period. This type of bankruptcy is also called a "reorganization," because the debtor eventually pays back much of his debt.

All types of bankruptcy have certain minimum requirements that must be met by the debtor in order for him or her to be eligible to file for bankruptcy relief. Any individual, even if self-employed or operating an unincorporated business, is eligible for Chapter 13 relief as long as the individual's unsecured debts are less than $383,175 and his or her secured debts are less than $1,149,525 (11 USC § 109(e)).

These amounts are adjusted periodically to reflect changes in the consumer price index. A corporation or partnership may not be a Chapter 13 debtor.

The bankruptcy trustee assigned to the case works with the court and the debtor to design a payment plan that will pay back a certain percentage of all outstanding debt each month. Under this plan, there are certain eligibility requirements for the debtors: consistent income and the ability to prove to the court that they can make the new payments outlined in the trustee's plan. The length of the repayment plan depends on how much income the debtor has and how much debt is owed.

What Happens to a House in a Chapter 13 Bankruptcy?

In Chapter 13, the borrower does not automatically lose the home. They can choose to retain the home and continue making mortgage payments. If the debtor wants to keep the collateral, securing a particular claim (in this case the home), the plan must provide that the holder of the secured claim (the noteholder) receives at least the value of the collateral. If the obligation underlying the secured claim was used to buy the collateral and the debt was incurred within certain time frames before the bankruptcy filing, the plan must provide for full payment of the debt, not just the value of the collateral (which may be less due to depreciation).

Payments to certain secured creditors (i.e., the mortgage lender), may be made over the original loan repayment schedule (which may be longer than the plan), so long as any arrearage is made up during the plan.

What Does Chapter 13 Bankruptcy Mean for Noteholders?

It can mean a few different things. During Chapter 13, a noteholder or lender typically still receives payments from the borrower. In order to remain in the home, the debtor will need to continue making payments on the mortgage. If mortgage payments are not made in a timely fashion, the lender can foreclose and sell the home after requesting and being granted a "motion for relief" from the court.

If the debtor fell behind on mortgage payments *prior* to filing a Chapter 13, he or she will need to pay off those arrears through the repayment plan created by the trustee. Because of this, the lender cannot foreclose on the home for prebankruptcy arrears as long as they are being paid off through the bankruptcy plan.

Chapter 13 bankruptcy may delay a foreclosure but will not permanently stop it. This costs a lot in terms of time, lost income, and frustration. The noteholder may also incur legal fees in order to defend their claim.

Under Certain Circumstances, Junior Liens Can Become Unsecured

Junior liens can be eliminated or wiped out if there is no equity to support them. The term "wiped" means the loan is no longer valid, and the lender can no longer collect or foreclose. This typically only happens in a Chapter 13, with a few exceptions. Let's look at an example. Suppose at the time a borrower files Chapter 13, the home is worth $200,000. It has two secured mortgages on it:

- Mortgage #1: $150,000 (Senior Loan)
- Mortgage #2: $25,000 (Junior Loan)

Total owed on the home: $175,000.

Since the home is worth $200,000, if the home was sold that day, there would be $25,000 of equity above what is owed to both noteholders. In this case, the junior lien *cannot* be wiped. Let's look at another example. The same home is worth $200,000.

- Mortgage #1: $200,000 (Senior Loan)
- Mortgage #2: $25,000 (Junior Loan)

In this example, the home has two secured mortgages on it. However, the value of the loans is greater than the value of the property. So in this situation, it is possible for the junior loan to be eliminated *if the borrower completes the Chapter 13 plan.* The borrower's attorney would need to file a motion to strip the lien with the court, and then the court would have to approve the motion. In addition, keep in mind this bankruptcy repayment plan is three to five years long. The borrower must *complete* the plan fully in order to strip a lien. Most borrowers do not complete Chapter 13 plans. I have heard varying statistics, but a rule of thumb is that somewhere in the range of 70–80 percent of all borrowers who enter into a Chapter 13 never complete their payoff plans. So while junior liens *can* be stripped, it is by no means a sure thing. Senior liens, on the other hand, cannot be stripped.

Bankruptcy is a complex proceeding. If you decide to purchase notes on a regular basis, I would encourage you to educate yourself on this topic. For more information, visit:

http://www.uscourts.gov/services-forms/bankruptcy/bankruptcy-basics/chapter-13-bankruptcy-basics
http://www.nolo.com/legal-encyclopedia/bankruptcy

How to Protect Your Investment

What happens if one of the notes I own falls behind on payments or stops paying altogether? I immediately reach out to the borrower with a letter or phone call. I try and communicate with them and genuinely try to understand what happened to their financial situation. Is this a short-term bump in the road? Is it an illness that they will recover from in just a month or two? Or has one of the borrowers lost a job and the payment on one income is just too much for them? After hearing their story and verifying the information, I run through many options available *before* deciding that foreclosure is the best option. **Oftentimes foreclosure is not the best option to pursue.**

For example, the noteholder has the power to modify a loan agreement—temporarily or permanently. I could lower the payment, reduce the interest rate, or simply forgive a payment to help get them caught up. If I determine they are unable or unwilling to pay, however, I can simply instruct my attorney to begin foreclosure proceedings and prepare to sell or rent the property. Each borrower's situation is different, so I make the judgment on a case-by-case basis.

I use my servicer or collection specialist to conduct all borrower communication on my behalf. This is because I am not a debt collector, and I would rather not talk with borrowers personally. This leaves me more free time to look for more deals. Plus, I just really want to avoid bringing negativity into my day and becoming emotionally involved in the transaction, which is oftentimes hard when your hard-earned money is at stake.

Again, I want to stress what we have covered here is not comprehensive. The laws vary greatly depending on where the property and the borrower are located. There are also legal and governmental disclosures protecting the borrower, timelines, and other paperwork involved that I have not discussed. This is an area you will need to study yourself to become familiar with the basics.

Always have a servicer and attorney involved and communicating on your behalf. *Never, ever try to do it yourself*, as this is a recipe for real problems. Find a competent professional and have them help you. This will enable you to remain compliant with all federal and state laws and keep your lien position protected.

In Summary

What we just covered is a bird's-eye view that addresses some of the frequently asked questions with regard to foreclosure and bankruptcy. You should now have a general idea of what happens during and after foreclosure and bankruptcy proceedings, as well as the basics of what to expect—minus the nitty-gritty details of each step.

CHAPTER NINE

HOW NOTES PROVIDE DIVERSIFICATION

The way to become rich is to put all your eggs in one basket and then watch that basket.
—Andrew Carnegie

One of the things I really love about notes is their ability to diversify investment. By this I don't mean across separate asset classes, like spreading your money between stocks, bonds, and real estate. What I'm referring to is the ability to spread capital over multiple notes to reduce your overall risk. When people think of buying a note, they often think of investing a large amount of money—$100,000 or more. This not always the case. You can buy a great note for between $10,000 and $20,000. This allows you spread your investment money over *multiple* motes. It provides stability and diversification because not all your eggs are in one basket. If one of the eggs breaks, you still have plenty to eat.

Let's use an example for reference. Suppose you have $100,000 sitting in your IRA, earning 3 percent (if you're lucky). You could do one of the following things:

- Buy one note for $100,000 (and expect to earn about 10 percent interest per year).
  OR
- Buy *five* notes for $20,000 each (and expect to earn about 10 percent interest per year).

Which would you rather have? I would prefer having the five notes in my portfolio, because **diversification provides safety.** If something goes wrong with my single $100,000 note, the income I receive could be delayed for months while I work things out with the borrower or foreclose. On the other hand, if something goes wrong with one of my five notes, I have four more depositing money each month like clockwork. It just makes good sense. This is one of the things I enjoy about note investing.

You can also further diversify by investing in notes of different types or classes. You can buy notes on residential properties (one to four units), commercial buildings (like office parks or strip malls), trailer parks, and even raw land. I personally prefer residential properties, but there are different notes that are just as lucrative if not more so.

Risk and Reward

A key financial concept is the idea of risk and reward. This is the idea that the more risk an investor is willing to take, the greater the potential reward should be. This is because investors need to be compensated for increased risk. More risk, more reward. Less risk, less reward. This is why credit card companies charge higher rates than mortgage companies.

The credit card company is an unsecured creditor, which is a risky position to be in as a lender. Because of this, they need to earn a higher reward in order to make taking that risk worthwhile.

Not all low-risk investments make sense. US Treasury securities are good examples. These are investments—such as bills, notes, and bonds that are debt obligations of the government. When you buy a US Treasury security, you are lending money to the federal government for a specified period.

From the general public's point of view, these are widely considered the safest form of investment. I personally disagree with this, as I don't have faith in our government or its financial system. However, the investment community as a whole has determined that there is little to no risk in buying US Treasury securities. And because they are considered almost no risk, they also pay investors *next to nothing*. So no risk, no real reward. Take a look at the current US Treasury rates of return, below. These change frequently but are current as of 2017.

Date	1 Mo	3 Mo	6 Mo	1 Yr	2 Yr	3 Yr
1/3/2017	0.52	0.53	0.56	0.89	1.22	1.50
1/4/2017	0.49	0.53	0.63	0.87	1.24	1.50
1/5/2017	0.51	0.52	0.62	0.83	1.17	1.43
1/6/2017	0.50	0.53	0.61	0.85	1.22	1.50
1/9/2017	0.50	0.50	0.60	0.82	1.21	1.47
1/10/2017	0.51	0.52	0.60	0.82	1.19	1.47
1/11/2017	0.51	0.52	0.60	0.82	1.20	1.47
1/12/2017	0.52	0.52	0.59	0.81	1.18	1.45
1/13/2017	0.52	0.53	0.61	0.82	1.21	1.48

You can see that by buying something with a rate of return this low, your money is not keeping up with inflation. This means you are *losing money* over time.

What Is the Right Balance of Risk and Reward?

As with many things in life, the answer is "it depends." Much of this will depend on your personal preference and investing comfort level, including how much money you have available to invest and when you plan on retiring.

The good news about buying notes is that **you can buy what pleases you.** Remember how we talked about different types of notes? They fall into three broad categories: performing, re-performing, and non-performing. In reality, these represent different classes of risk and reward.

Performing Note

This is a note paying as agreed, so it's typically low risk. The buyer has never defaulted or even been more than thirty days late on their payment. Buying a note like this is very easy. You purchase it, take ownership, and begin collecting the mortgage payment from the borrower each month. There is virtually nothing else you need to do. Because this is more of a "turnkey" or passive scenario, your yield will be lower than with more active forms of note investing. However, this is still a great investment and yields can be in the double digits if you structure the purchase correctly.

Re-performing Note

With this asset, the borrower stopped paying at some point in the past. The noteholder may have worked out a loan modification or agreement to help get the borrower repaying again. After the borrower has resumed payments for a few months, the note can be called "re-performing." Now the borrower is back on track and paying as agreed. To be considered a re-performing note, payments must have been made on time for a minimum of the past six to twelve months. This is where you can find really good deals, since there is a little bit of risk because the borrower has been delinquent before. But they have also been back on track. Good deals can be found with re-performing assets.

Non-performing Note

These are notes where the borrower has "fallen off the horse." They are no longer paying as agreed. They may have stopped paying last month, five months ago, or three years ago. Because the loan is in default, certain measures need to be taken to work something out with the borrower. This can mean modifying the loan to help them resume payments, or recovering the property from them through legal action. Although investing in non-performing notes may sound like disaster for an investor, there are extremely good deals to be had in this area. This is because you can buy defaulted loans for *steep discounts*. Pennies on the dollar, in many cases.

I frequently purchase this asset class. I do so because I have experience, expertise, and tools at my disposal. The returns are also quite high. So high, in fact, that it makes the risk of buying them worthwhile. Each investor will have a business model for this area, but frequently the plan is to buy the note at a steep discount, then reach out to the borrower to begin collections. In my model, we work with the borrower to modify the loan. This results in a much better deal for the borrower than the loan terms they had previously. The newly modified note is at a much lower rate, a lower payment, and overall better terms than the original. We are working with the borrowers to help them keep their homes. To invest in non-performing notes, it's a good idea to have many options and exit strategies thought out in advance. We can let our attorney or collections specialist pursue the legal route and begin foreclosure, or work with the borrower and simply modify the note.

Because we have purchased the note at such a steep discount, we have a huge amount of room to forgive debt and modify the loan terms. Investors can buy first or second mortgages in this manner. The learning curve is *steep*, however, and beyond the scope of this book. Suffice it to say this is an area where risk and reward definitely come into play. To the outsider, it might seem crazy to buy assets like this. Once you have mastered that original learning curve, though, it becomes easy to see how to manipulate the risk and make small bets, so that any one deal will not clean you out. Overall, the gains from this model are far above average.

Here are a few general exit strategies and ways to profit when collecting on non-performing notes. These strategies come into play once contact with the borrower(s) has been made. Making contact with them is the hardest part of the process. Keep in mind also that this list is very general in nature.

There are many more nuances that should be considered prior to buying or collecting on a non-performing asset.

Non-performing Note Exit Strategies (Ways to Profit)

- reinstate loan in full and have the borrower make payments according to original promissory note

- payment plan (forbearance)
- loan modification
- discounted payoff
- sales assistance (sell the home)
- short sale
- foreclosure
- deed in lieu of foreclosure
- foreclose, then rent the property

Here is an important thing to remember. **The more experience and education an investor has, the less risk he experiences in real-life investments.** Many investing topics, like buying non-performing notes, have a steep learning curve, but once the investor masters the field, the risk is manageable because he knows what to look for and the proper due diligence to perform when evaluating potential purchases. This education and real-world experience help him manipulate or minimize risk. (This applies to all forms of investing.)

I personally buy a mix of non-performing and performing notes. I love them both for the steady cash flow. In case you are wondering, it is actually beneficial for all parties involved—including the borrower—to work out a payment plan or some form of assistance when a loan is in default. Foreclosing is a last resort and may not be the best outcome.

Risk Tolerance: What Is Yours?

Risk tolerance is a concept most people understand intuitively. What one person considers risky may feel safe to another. Most people are most concerned with **recovering their money and avoiding loss.** Second, we want our money to be earning a rate of return. And last but not least, we want our money to be earning as much as possible.

Primary Concerns

1. protecting my money (safety and wealth preservation).
2. growing my money (increasing wealth over time).
3. getting the highest return I can (while still adhering to #1).

Which of the three are most important to *you*? No doubt all are important to some extent, but I'm sure one stands out above the rest.

Understanding what you consider "risky" will go a long way in helping decide your investment choices. Do you find you rank #3 as the most important? If so, you are probably more comfortable with higher levels of calculated risk.

The next chapter discusses how to calculate yield using a financial calculator. It may not be exciting, but it's the best way to determine if your note deal makes good financial sense.

CHAPTER TEN

HOW TO CALCULATE YIELD FOR YOURSELF

Formal education will make you a living. Self-education will make you a fortune.
—Jim Rohn Entrepreneur and business teacher

What and Why

This chapter explains yield. It is a rather important subject, because buying a note at a discount—even a steep one—does not guarantee a certain yield or return. They are two very separate things. Remember, as mentioned, **yield is the interest rate your money is earning on an annualized basis.** In most note transactions, whether you're buying, selling, or holding one for cash flow, using yield as the method of measurement is almost always the best metric to decide whether the investment was a wise one.

Yield is the ideal way to calculate the return on note investments because it takes into account both the time value of money (TVM) and interest.

Why Is Knowing Yield Important?

Being able to effectively calculate yield will increase your financial knowledge—and also elevate you into the realm of the few folks who actually know what their investments are earning. **Yield is different from other calculations such as ROI, Cash-on-Cash, and Internal Rate of Return.** Many people mistakenly believe that because they buy a note at a large discount the yield will automatically be high. This is incorrect. While a discount is great when you can get one, don't get hung up on the amount of the discount. Focus on the yield. Several things can influence the yield on a note:

- interest rate
- payment amount
- number of payments remaining
- purchase price (price you are paying)
- method of amortizing (if it has a balloon at some point)

Changing even one of the above variables slightly can and will change the yield *drastically*. This is important for you to know as buyer, seller, or investor. As you may imagine, yield can be challenging to calculate by hand. Fortunately, there is a much easier way. You can do all this with a good old-fashioned financial calculator. There are many newer models available, but I'm going to show you the one I am most familiar with. It's called the HP12C, and it's made by Hewlett-Packard. I'm not going to lie: it's an old-looking machine and not very sexy. In fact, it has been around (and very popular) for over twenty years. There are other, much newer models on the market now, but this is what I know inside and out, so I will be using this one. Incidentally, you can also download an app from iTunes that is an exact replica of this calculator. It's inexpensive, and you can carry it with you on your phone or tablet.

Sexy, Right?

OK, so maybe not. But this thing will answer all your yield questions. It was actually quite difficult for me to learn how to calculate yield, as there are very few good step-by-step sources on how to calculate it by hand. I am fairly sure you didn't start reading this book for extra math practice, so let's get this over with and just get you a good working knowledge. After a few exercises, you will understand the basics and will be able to practice more on your own on an as-needed basis. And just so you know, before I started using this calculator I knew virtually nothing about finance calculators. I say that to reassure you. Once you understand the basics, it's really not that hard at all.

So to start, you will need to buy an HP12C. Or you can download the app for your IOS, iPhone, or iPad. Both perform the same functions and work very well.

Keys You Don't Use

Looking at the calculator, you will notice a lot of very foreign-looking keys. Ignore almost all of them. This thing is pretty powerful and meant to do many things other than yield calculations, so we only use a few of the keys and functions. On the lower left you will see the "On" button. Punch it once to turn the device on, once more to turn it off. It will also turn itself off if left on long enough so it won't drain the battery.

The Five Financial Keys

Here are the keys we *will* use to determine yield. Once you become familiar with them, it's really a piece of cake. Looking at the calculator, in the upper left row, you'll see five keys. These are the primary keys we will be using. Here is what each represents:

N = Number of Payments
I = Interest, or Yield/Return
PV = Present Value
PMT = Payment
FV = Future Value

Don't be put off by all this calculating stuff. It's really easy. You can make things even easier on yourself by drawing a table to fill in the blanks for your problem. Take a moment and get a blank sheet of paper and draw a table that looks like this:

N	I	PV	PMT	FV

Before we do a couple of practice problems, let's look at the five calculator keys and what they really mean in layman's terms.

N = Number of Payments

This is expressed as a monthly amount. A note with a thirty-year term is expressed as 360. If the same note has only twenty-five years remaining, then you enter the number 300 and press the "n" button. Remember, the term—or N key—will always be *expressed in months, not years*. This key is where you enter the **remaining amount of months left on the note.**

I = Interest, Yield, or Return

When buying a note, I save this field for last. It can be used a variety of ways, but it reveals the yield an investment will produce for you—or any buyer. One thing to remember is that "i," the interest rate button, will only show you interest on a *monthly* basis. Whatever answer it produces you simply multiply by twelve months. So if it says "1.5," you multiply by twelve months and you see the yearly yield is 18 percent.

PV = Present Value

Present value can be used in several ways, both in buying and selling. When you're buying a note, the present value stands for the *purchase price*, which is the amount you may be buying the note for. This is always entered as a *negative number*. Here's an example. Suppose you are considering buying a note for $20,000. This would represent the present value. You type in 20000 and then press the "CHS" key. Then press the "PV" key. You will notice when pressing the "CHS" key it converts the sum into a negative number. Not to worry, that's exactly what it's supposed to do. It becomes a negative number because this is a money *outlay* or cost.

PMT = Payment

This is where you enter the note payment amount. This is the monthly payment from the borrower. If the total monthly payment (both principal and interest) is $350, then you would type the numbers "350" and then press the "PMT" key.

You do *not* include taxes or insurance that may be included in the monthly payment. Only the principal and interest portion of the payment are used.

FV = Future Value

This is used in situations where a loan is not expected to amortize fully. This could be an interest-only loan or a balloon. A balloon is a situation where the principal and interest payments do not pay off the loan in full at the end of the term. The borrower would need to come up with a lump sum, or "balloon," to finish paying the remaining balance on the loan.

If there is no balloon, simply press zero, then the "FV" key. If there is a balloon of say $30,000, simply press 30000 then the "FV" key.

Keep in mind that you can enter any of the above five keys *in any order*. It really does not matter what order you do the calculation in. You can enter them backward or forward, left to right, or right to left. You can sometimes even leave out a key or two and still get the correct answer!

I have highlighted in red the only keys we really use. Of course we use the number keys as well, but that's pretty much it. I will show you the basics on each of these and how to calculate yield for yourself on a variety of deals.

Don't Worry about Getting It Right

The calculator stores the information you enter, so don't fret. If you ever need to cancel and start over, simply hit the yellow "f" key and then the "CLX" key. That clears all the registers so you can start over.

Yield Practice Example #1: Buying a Note

Let's try an example together. A seller is offering you a note for purchase. He wants you to make him an offer. You, being a smart investor, know you want to be earning a 10 percent yield with your invested dollars. So you need to punch a few numbers to determine the price you are willing to pay.

The seller provides you with the following information about the note:

Unpaid Principal Balance: $63,000
Term: 30 years
Remaining Payments: 204
Interest Rate: 5.5%
Monthly Payment: $357.71
Balloon: None

Get out your trusty calculator and enter the following:

- In the N column, we put the remaining payments we are buying: 204. So type in 204 and press the "n" key.

N	I	PV	PMT	FV
204				

- Now, since we want to earn a 10 percent yield, enter the number 10 on the keypad, then press the blue "g" key, then the "i" key. This will show you a number of 0.83333 (this is the monthly rate).

N	I	PV	PMT	FV
204	0.83333			

- Next enter the payment, which is $357.71. Then press the "PMT" key.

N	I	PV	PMT	FV
204	0.83333		357.71	

- There is no balloon on this note, so we press zero and then press the "FV" key. If you have been following along and writing in your table as suggested, it should look like this:

N	I	PV	PMT	FV
204	0.83333		357.71	0

So where is our answer? Well it's hidden in the "PV" key. Press "PV" now for the *exact dollar amount* you should pay the seller to receive your 10 percent yield annually. Did you get –35,028.03?

N	I	PV	PMT	FV
204	0.83333	–35,028.03	357.71	0

You will notice it shows up as a *negative* number. This is because it is a cash outflow (from your pocket to the seller's). This is the exact dollar amount to buy the note for, to ensure this investment earns a 10 percent yield. Now I would suggest, at least initially, offering a lower amount. This will give you room to negotiate with the seller. In almost every transaction, there will be some back-and-forth negotiation. If you start your offer at the exact max price you are willing to pay, you have left yourself no negotiating room.

However, if you start lower, the seller will inevitably want more, and you are more likely to arrive at the price you really wanted, which is closer to $35,028.03.

Yield Practice Example #2: Buying a Note with a Balloon

You are thinking about buying a note that has a balloon payment. The seller needs to sell quickly and needs your offer in the next twenty-four hours. Here's the information he provided you:

Unpaid Principal Balance: $37,428
Term: 15 years
Remaining Payments: 156
Interest Rate: 6%
Monthly Payment: $315.84

Balloon: $15,000 due from borrower at end of fifteen-year term.

Again, let's turn to our trusty calculator.

- Just like in the previous exercise, we put the remaining term in the N column. So type in "156" and press the "n" key.

N	I	PV	PMT	FV
156				

- Let's say we decide this note is risky for one reason or another, and to make it worth getting involved, we would like to earn a 12 percent yield. Remember, it's really up to *you* to decide. Go ahead and press the number "12" on the keypad, then press the blue "g" key, then press the "i" key. This will show you a number of 1.00 (again, this is the monthly rate).

N	I	PV	PMT	FV
156	1.00			

- Next, enter the payment amount, which is 315.84. Then press the "PMT" key.

N	I	PV	PMT	FV
156	1.00		315.84	

- There is a balloon of $15,000 on this note, so enter 15000 and then press the "FV" key. At this point, your table should look like this:

N	I	PV	PMT	FV
156	1.00		315.84	15,000

So what is the purchase price you need to offer the seller to be earning 12 percent annually on this note? Remember, it does have a balloon, but that has been factored in. Press the "PV" key on your calculator now for the answer.

And there you have it! The exact amount is $28,071.99. See how easy this is?

N	I	PV	PMT	FV
156	1.00	–28,071.99	315.84	15,000

Yield Practice Example #3: Modifying a Note

In this example, we will assume you somehow got your hands on a non-performing note. This could have been a note you already own that was performing but then stopped, or one you purchased with the plan of modifying the borrower's terms. Remember how I briefly mentioned that when buying non-performing notes, the goal is typically to work with the borrower to modify the loan at a lower rate and payment.

This helps the borrower afford the payment and, because you would have been able to purchase the loan at a steep discount, still gives you a great yield.

Here are the current loan details. Remember, in this scenario the borrower has *stopped* paying. They still owe the money. Let's also assume in this example that you have contacted them and they are willing to stay in the home and keep making payments—provided you can modify the loan to something more affordable. Here is what they currently owe:

Unpaid Principal Balance: $89,125
Term: 20 years
Remaining Payments: 200
Interest Rate: 8%
Monthly Payment: $745.48
Balloon: None

Given the time and expense of modifying the note, you will want to determine the minimum yield you will accept. Let's say you want 16 percent. Based on the loan information, what payment does the borrower need to be making in order for you to receive that yield? Remember, as a lender, when you modify a note any of the terms can be changed—provided the borrower agrees to them.

- Let's get out our calculator and run some numbers. In this example, I would simply start over with a new twenty-year loan term. You could of course make the term anything you want. Type in "240" and press the "n" key.

N	I	PV	PMT	FV
240				

- Next, type in the interest rate, or yield you want to be earning. Press the numbers "16" on the keypad, then press the blue "g" key, then press the "i" key. This will show you a number of 1.33 (again, this is the monthly rate).

N	I	PV	PMT	FV
240	1.33333			

- Next, we will want to determine what you originally paid for the note. This would be your acquisition price, also called your "basis" in the note. This could be any number, but let's assume for this example it's $38,000. Press the numbers 38,000 on the keypad, then press the "CHS" key. Again, you will see this is a negative number, –38000. Now press the "PV" key.

N	I	PV	PMT	FV
240	1.33333	–38000		

- In this example, there is no balloon payment, so the simply type zero on your keypad and press the "FV" key.

N	I	PV	PMT	FV
240	1.33333	-38000		0

You can see we performed this calculation a little differently, but it still shows us the yield. In this case, we entered all the information we had access to, and **asked the calculator to tell us what the payment should be in order for us to achieve a 16 percent yield.**

- For the final step press, the "PMT" key for the answer. You should have a payment of $528.67. This is the amount the borrower will need to pay each month for you to modify the loan and receive a 16 percent yield.

N	I	PV	PMT	FV
240	1.33333	–38000	$528.67	0

It turns out this is a lower payment than the borrower originally had, and a win for you. Obviously, you can change other variables such as the term, price you paid, and interest rate. These can all be manipulated to come up with loan terms that are profitable for you and that will make sense for the borrower.

I hope you see how powerful calculating yield can be, as it opens the door to extraordinary profits. Begin playing with these calculations and continue to study on your own to improve. If you are looking for more in-depth calculator tutorials, send me an e-mail. I'm happy to point you to other resources.

CHAPTER ELEVEN

HOW YOU CAN GET STARTED

The way to learn to do things is to do things. Success teaches how to succeed. Begin with determination to succeed, and the work is half done already.
—Unknown

We have covered very basic information so far. You should now have a general understanding of the opportunity and financial benefits notes can provide.

So how do you get started? What are the next steps? **The first step is to stop and ask yourself what your financial goals are**. I find most people skip the planning stage but rush out and dabble—with real money. They try this and that, never taking enough time to really become actually good at something. They don't decide what it is they *really* want in their financial life. They bounce around from shiny object to shiny object: house flipping, tax liens, real-estate investing, stock trading. It can go on and on. I know; I did this myself for a long time.

The concept to understand is that **investments are just tools.** Financial tools used to reach milestones and goals in your life. They can be used to achieve financial freedom, possibly quit your day job, and become a full-time investor, or to grow a portfolio for retirement.

So before you jump headlong into buying notes, begin with the end in mind. What do you want your financial life to look like in three, five, or ten years? How much money should your portfolio be generating on an annual basis, and what should your life look like? Knowing the answers to these questions is important because it allows you to gauge where you are now and where you want to be. It will also show you where the holes are in your plan. You will begin to see the skills you lack or may need to acquire in order to reach your goals. If the skills are so complex that they would take many years or even a lifetime to master, you can likely outsource them to people who already have that specialized skill set. Leverage other experts whenever you can.

When asked about investing goals, most people often have a vague answer. Something along the lines of "I want to make money." To me, that's not much of a plan. It's more of a wish. It's not strong enough or emotional enough to matter to them when the going gets tough.

Be more specific. Ask questions like:

- Why am I investing?
- Why is it important to me?
- How much money do I need?
- What will the money do for me?
- How will I know when I've succeeded?

Most important, ask yourself the question: "What skills or character traits do I need to learn or to acquire in order to reach my goals?"

Having a well-thought-out plan—including your *why* for doing it—will take you a long way toward completing your goals. Simply saying you want to make some extra money is not sufficient. Get clear on the details, write them down, and review them often.

I am a firm believer in written goals. I read and rewrite my goals daily. I believe goals need to have the following qualities in order to be successful in the long term:

1. **Have a Why.** Have a strong "why," or emotional reason deeply important to you.

2. **Be Actionable.** There must be daily or weekly actions in place to move the goal forward.

3. **Be Measurable.** Goals must be tracked and measured. This lets you know if you are making progress or if a course adjustment is needed.

And finally, you need to be *persistent.* I'm not talking about beating your head against a wall unnecessarily if something is not working. If something repeatedly isn't working, then *quit doing it.* That's just foolishness. The kind of persistence I'm talking about is used to push you through the hard and frustrating times to get things done, because what you are working on is **important to you at a deep level.**

I'd like to point out one thing about goals. You don't need to have all the details figured out in advance. You only need to be clear on what you want and be 100 percent emotionally invested in making that outcome happen. Then take daily actions toward that goal. That's it.

The details will come as you start working on your plan. That's part of the learning process. You will adjust course many times before you reach your destination.

What Type of Investor Are You?

After you have taken the time to think about your investing goals, the next step is to determine what kind of investor you are. Most investors fall into one of two categories: *active* or *passive.*

Passive Investor

A person who makes the initial investment choice, applies money toward an investment, and then trusts others to manage the day-to-day operations. A passive investor is typically not making day-to-day decisions and is not concerned with daily management. This is usually someone who has a day job, a family, or otherwise a full schedule outside of investing. **This is a legitimate investor who may be well educated but who does not have time or the inclination to locate or manage investments on a full-time basis.**

Active Investor

A person who applies an active strategy of buying, selling, and managing investments. They also make regular investment decisions, and they tend to do a lot of research. In real estate, this would be someone who manages properties, negotiates deals, develops vendor relationships, and sets rents. **This usually is a person who focuses on investing full time.**

Depending on the type of investor you are, there will be different opportunities available. If you are an active investor, you may benefit from learning and studying everything you can get your hands on and then doing a few deals with a trusted advisor or mentor. You may plan to get more involved later on, through joint venture or partnership deals, or even by starting your own investment fund to manage both your own and other people's investments.

If you are a passive investor, there is good news. You don't need to quit your job or learn a new trade to make money with notes. In fact, investing is relatively easy once you know the basics. There are many coaching and partnership programs available, in addition to what is called an "investment fund." As mentioned previously, an investment fund is essentially a company formed to pool money together and buy assets. Many times these assets are notes, real estate, or stocks.

A properly organized fund will follow and adhere to all state and federal guidelines and securities laws.

Investment Fund

A fund can be structured an almost unlimited amount of ways, so long as it adheres to securities law. These laws fall under the US Securities and Exchange Commission guidelines. Investors buy shares of a fund. This means they have real ownership in the company but no day-to-day decision-making control. Managers of the fund are typically experienced and seasoned investors with a track record.

Managers leverage their investing expertise to help the fund realize a profit. This can be structured in many ways, from sharing of equity in the deals to an interest rate paid to investors on all the invested money. Many popular models include a preferred rate of return for investors, somewhere between 8 and 12 percent. This means investors are paid an interest rate of 8–12 percent on their invested money. At the end of the investment term, they are given their principal amount back, or they can reinvest it. The term is usually two to five years but can be any time frame agreed to. This is a great way for the passive investor to piggyback on an expert's experience and to earn above-average returns.

To be eligible to participate in an investment fund, investors need to be either an **accredited or sophisticated investor.**

Accredited Investor

In the United States, to be considered an accredited investor, you must have a net worth of at least one million US dollars—excluding the value of your primary residence—or have had income of at least $200,000 each year for the past two years (or $300,000 combined income, if married). You must have the expectation that you will make the same amount the following year.

OR

You must be a bank, insurance company, charitable organization, corporation, or partnership with assets exceeding five million dollars.

Sophisticated Investor

In the United States, the definition of a sophisticated investor is a little ambiguous. Instead of exact income and net worth requirements, it is broadly defined as an investor with sufficient knowledge and experience in financial and business matters to make that person capable of evaluating the merits and risks of the prospective investment.

In broad terms, this means the investor must be able to think for himself, and he or she must be financially savvy. This is obviously open to interpretation—suffice it to say it is not wise to take Grandma's last $10,000 and put it into an investment fund, no matter how "safe" that fund may appear to be.

Buy a Note and Collect the Income!

Both active and passive investors can buy individual notes and simply hold them for income. Since they make ideal investments for a self-directed IRA, buying notes for long-term hold is a great strategy for many investors. It is hard to beat steady—even boring—returns that aren't subject to the ups and downs of the stock market.

While there is tremendous opportunity, finding suitable deals that meet your investing criteria may be harder to come by than you think. Everyone is looking for a great deal. This is why **it's important to create relationships with people who can help.** No man is an island, and getting people on your team like brokers, mentors, or fund managers will be one of the keys to your success. If you are buying just one note or two, you probably don't need to establish much in the way of relationships. However, if you are planning on being a full-time investor in notes, you should spend time cultivating the beneficial relationships.

Understand that there is **no shortage of deals.** If you can't find them, you need to cultivate relationships with people who can point you to them.

There are plenty of deals to be had, but as with anything it takes effort and time to sort the wheat from the chaff. **Avoid trying to do it all alone.** The three most expensive words in the English language are "Do it yourself." If you are confused where to start, feel free to reach out to me. I can give you resources to study, and I can connect you with people who should be able to help, depending on your investment needs. Also see the resources section of this book for further reading.

Possible "Next Steps" for Investors of Both Types

For the Passive Investor

Simply study and learn as much as possible. Then invest with other full-time investors through a joint venture, partnership, or investment fund. You can also purchase performing notes on a single, one-off basis for your self-directed IRA. This is the easiest way to get involved with a very low time commitment. But study up first. Do your due diligence regarding the people involved. Start with a small deal to get your feet wet. There is no rush, so don't put all your eggs in one basket. Take it slow. Buy one small note, get familiar with how the transaction works, and read all the associated documents. Then if you like it, buy another. It really is that easy.

For the Active Investor

I suggest, initially at least, partnering or working with a mentor who already has connections and resources to share. Typically, this comes with strings attached. Be prepared to do some grunt work or offer your mentor value in return in some way. Don't expect someone to hand you years of hard-earned experience for free. My first mentor was a workout specialist in the non-performing space. We met through a referral, and I paid him to help me with my non-performing notes. This opened many doors for me—and developed into a great friendship. This kind of arrangement is what you should seek. You want to be "riding shotgun," seeing the deals and how the mentor approaches them. Securing a relationship like this is *invaluable*. It will shorten your learning curve and help you avoid a great deal of frustration.

Be aware that securing a relationship with a mentor might not be easy. It will take time and dedication. Focus on providing value to your mentor. Don't ask—give instead. Help that person with his or her business however you can, and it will open doors for yours. **Approach them with the mind-set of trying to help them first and yourself second.**

It's important to mention here that I am not referring to a paid training course, although those can be useful. Use discretion with paid education, as you can pay thousands for a course that only offers very basic training and little hands-on experience. I believe securing a genuine mentor for yourself is a better avenue for success.

Choosing the Right Partner or Mentor

I am a firm believer in education. Not formal, school-type education, but real-world education that helps us make sound choices. I believe that before you can partner or invest with someone you need to do your homework and ultimately know your investment model inside out and the people involved. Just because you have a day job doesn't mean you shouldn't be well educated on the risks or rewards of a particular investment. Study, read all you can, and ask questions. Don't assume others will have your best interests at heart. Get to know whom you are investing with on a personal level.

Only invest your money with someone after you have spent enough time educating yourself that you feel like you are ready to make an informed decision. In this manner, you can also take on some level of personal responsibility, fully understand the business model, and appreciate whom you are investing with. Education also serves to protect you from deals or people who may not be aligned with your goals.

Ask yourself these questions:

1. Can this person be trusted?
2. Are they an expert in their field?
3. Do they have experience in this specific endeavor and a verifiable track record?

If the answer to all three is yes, then you are probably in good hands.

In Closing, a Quick Story about My "Why" for Investing

Here is why attaining financial freedom is important to *me*. Something happened to me while I was writing this book that drove home why I invest.

When I was ten years old, my parents moved our family from a big city in California to a small town in northern Idaho. They purchased twenty acres in the mountains, which was far away from neighbors. The property was secluded, forested, and pretty remote. Our nearest neighbor was more than two miles away. I remember that our house was exactly 4.8 miles from the paved road. One winter we had more than nine feet of snow and had to snowmobile to school.

This is how my two younger brothers and I grew up. As children and into our teens, we learned the value of hard work and persistence. We helped our father plant more than a hundred fruit trees and several gardens, most of which are still there today. We helped dig a pond and stock it with fish, cut and stack firewood for winter, and much more. We had fun, too. We rode horses, went hunting and exploring, played in the woods, and learned to relax and be at peace with nature. It was an excellent way to grow up, and I am very thankful my parents chose to raise us that way.

Recently, I took a trip to visit my parents. They still live where I grew up. My mother brought out several large scrapbooks filled with photos. It was amazing to see how much we had changed, and all the photos of our experiences together.

Suddenly, my father stopped and pointed to one picture. It was of the two of us standing next to a stream. He had a big cowboy hat on. I must have been about ten years old in the photo. He said, "Out of all our pictures, this is my favorite of us together." I'm not sure why that picture meant so much to him, but I could tell he was serious. For some reason, his comment stuck with me.

As the trip neared a close and I was preparing to head back home, we stopped and took another picture together, in the exact same spot by the stream—well over twenty years after the first picture was taken.

This experience drives home why investing is important to me. We never know how much time we have left to spend with loved ones and family. And time, as they say, is money. It costs money to have free time. A majority of the population grinds away at jobs they hate, spending their days with people they don't like, just to earn a living. I don't want that. I want more time with family and friends. Time to do the things I enjoy.

Time for trips, good coffee, and reading. And maybe a good bottle of merlot. For me, investing is not about buying shinier, more expensive things.

It's about buying time.

CHAPTER TWELVE

CASE STUDIES AND REAL WORLD EXAMPLES

"If you want to be successful, you've got to develop the discipline not to let anything take your focus off the important things that will get results."
— John Addison

Many people new to investing are curious to see what actual note deals look like. This is a realistic expectation, because it's hard to wrap our head around the opportunity without seeing it for ourselves. Here are just a few from my personal experiences. Depending on the money you have available, risk tolerance and deal flow, your experience will be different.

You may notice something about these case studies. I like to make *small bets*. I prefer to invest a maximum of $10,000 to $40,000 in any one deal. That helps ensure that I don't have any single deal cleaning me out financially should something not go as planned. This helps spread risk to multiple deals and makes things safer. It's that "sleep good at night" feeling.

Case Study #1
Performing 1st Position Lien, MI

- Performing 1st Position Lien.
- Property FMV: $60,000.
- Senior Lien Amount: $54,973.47.
- Borrower pays us $412.08 per month.

Purchase price: $24,500. This equals 44.56% of UPB. This is also 49% of actual property value.

The Results: This loan was purchased performing, we just collect the check.

- **ROI: 20.38%**
- **Annualized Yield: 20%**
- **Annual Cash-Flow: $4,944.96**
- **Time from Purchase to Receiving Payments = 15 days.**

Here is what the amortization schedule looks like.

Case Study #1						
Compound Period: Monthly						
Nominal Annual Rate: 7.500 %						
CASH FLOW DATA						
	Event	**Date**	**Amount**	**Number**	**Period**	**End Date**
1	Loan	12/1/2016	54,973.47	1		
2	Payment	1/1/2017	412.08	288	Monthly	**12/1/2040**
AMORTIZATION SCHEDULE - Normal Amortization						
	Date	**Payment**	**Interest**	**Principal**	**Balance**	
Loan	12/1/2016				$ 54,973.47	
2016 Totals		0	0	0		
1	1/1/2017	$ 412.08	$ 343.58	$ 68.50	$ 54,904.97	
2	2/1/2017	$ 412.08	$ 343.16	$ 68.92	$ 54,836.05	
3	3/1/2017	$ 412.08	$ 342.73	$ 69.35	$ 54,766.70	
4	4/1/2017	$ 412.08	$ 342.29	$ 69.79	$ 54,696.91	
5	5/1/2017	$ 412.08	$ 341.86	$ 70.22	$ 54,626.69	
6	6/1/2017	$ 412.08	$ 341.42	$ 70.66	$ 54,556.03	
7	7/1/2017	$ 412.08	$ 340.98	$ 71.10	$ 54,484.93	
8	8/1/2017	$ 412.08	$ 340.53	$ 71.55	$ 54,413.38	
9	9/1/2017	$ 412.08	$ 340.08	$ 72.00	$ 54,341.38	
10	10/1/2017	$ 412.08	$ 339.63	$ 72.45	$ 54,268.93	
11	11/1/2017	$ 412.08	$ 339.18	$ 72.90	$ 54,196.03	
12	12/1/2017	$ 412.08	$ 338.73	$ 73.35	$ 54,122.68	
2017 Totals		**$ 4,944.96**	**$ 4,094.17**	**$ 850.79**		
288	12/1/2040	$ 412.08	0.53-	$ 412.61		0
2040 Totals		$ 4,944.96	$ 192.26	$ 4,752.70		
Grand Totals		**$ 118,679.04**	**$ 63,705.57**	**$ 54,973.47**		

Case Study #2
Non-Performing 2nd Position Lien, CA

- Non-Performing 2nd Lien.
- Property FMV: $360,000.
- Senior Lien Amount: $238,000.
- Senior Lien Status: Current, paid as agreed.

We purchased the 2nd lien with the intention of modifying the loan for the borrower. There was equity in the property and we had multiple exit strategies for this deal.

- 2nd Lien UPB: $63,327
- Our Purchase Price: $14,600
- Our Expenses: $700
- Our Total Investment: $15,300

The Results: Contacted borrower, willing to do a loan modification. Gave us $1,000 down payment to begin. Loan modified at 4% for 25-year term. Borrower pays us $334.26 per month.

- **ROI: 28.04%**
- **Annualized Yield: 24%**
- **Annual Cash-Flow: $4,011.12**
- **Time from Purchase to Receiving Payments = 3 months.**

Here is what the amortization schedule looks like.

Case Study #2						
Compound Period: Monthly						
Nominal Annual Rate: 4.000 %						
CASH FLOW DATA						
	Event	**Date**	**Amount**	**Number**	**Period**	**End Date**
1	Loan	12/1/2016	$ 63,327.00	1		
2	Payment	1/1/2017	$ 334.26	300	Monthly	**12/1/2041**
AMORTIZATION SCHEDULE - Normal Amortization						
	Date	**Payment**	**Interest**	**Principal**	**Balance**	
Loan	12/1/2016				$ 63,327.00	
2016 Totals		0	0	0		
1	1/1/2017	$ 334.26	$ 211.09	$ 123.17	$ 63,203.83	
2	2/1/2017	$ 334.26	$ 210.68	$ 123.58	$ 63,080.25	
3	3/1/2017	$ 334.26	$ 210.27	$ 123.99	$ 62,956.26	
4	4/1/2017	$ 334.26	$ 209.85	$ 124.41	$ 62,831.85	
5	5/1/2017	$ 334.26	$ 209.44	$ 124.82	$ 62,707.03	
6	6/1/2017	$ 334.26	$ 209.02	$ 125.24	$ 62,581.79	
7	7/1/2017	$ 334.26	$ 208.61	$ 125.65	$ 62,456.14	
8	8/1/2017	$ 334.26	$ 208.19	$ 126.07	$ 62,330.07	
9	9/1/2017	$ 334.26	$ 207.77	$ 126.49	$ 62,203.58	
10	10/1/2017	$ 334.26	$ 207.35	$ 126.91	$ 62,076.67	
11	11/1/2017	$ 334.26	$ 206.92	$ 127.34	$ 61,949.33	
12	12/1/2017	$ 334.26	$ 206.50	$ 127.76	$ 61,821.57	
2017 Totals		**4,011.12**	**2,505.69**	**1,505.43**		

300	12/1/2041	$ 334.26	0.48-	$ 334.74		0
2041 Totals		$ 4,011.12	$ 84.05	$ 3,927.07		
Grand Totals		**$ 100,278.00**	**$ 36,951.00**	**$ 63,327.00**		

Now that the loan is performing, we can sell on the open market to investors for around **$31,737 today.** Or, we can hold it long-term for cash-flow.

Case Study #3
Non-Performing 2nd Position Lien, MA

- Non-Performing 2nd Lien.
- Property FMV: $345,000.
- Senior Lien Amount: $235,289.
- Senior Lien Status: Current, paid as agreed.

We purchased the 2nd lien with the intention of modifying the loan for the borrower. There was equity in the property and we had multiple exit strategies for this deal.

- 2nd Lien UPB: $67,163
- Our Purchase Price: $15,111
- Our Expenses: $7,699
- Our Total Investment: $22,810

The Results: Contacted borrower, not cooperative. We foreclosed and took ownership of the home via the deed. Borrower decided they wanted to stay, and purchased deed back from us for $47,000 lump-sum payment.

- **ROI: 206%**
- **Annualized Yield: (not applicable)**
- **Annual Cash-Flow: (not applicable)**
- **Time from Purchase to Receiving Profit = 24 months.**

In this instance the borrower did not want to create a new note, or make payments. They simply preferred to pay a discounted lump-sum payment and to move on. Money like this is used to purchase more performing notes.

Case Study #4
Non-Performing 2nd Position Lien, MA

- Non-Performing 2nd Lien.
- Property FMV: $325,000.
- Senior Lien Amount: $217,000.
- Senior Lien Status: Current, paid as agreed.

We purchased the 2nd lien with the intention of modifying the loan for the borrower. There was equity in the property and we had multiple exit strategies for this deal.

- 2nd Lien UPB: $107,000
- Our Purchase Price: $13,100
- Our Expenses: $2,290
- Our Total Investment: $15,390

The Results: Contacted borrower, they were willing to do a loan modification. Gave us $7,500 down payment to begin. Loan modified at 4.5% for 30-year term. Borrower pays us $544.46 per month.

- **ROI: 82.80%**
- **Annualized Yield: 84%**
- **Annual Cash-Flow: $6,533.52**
- **Time from Purchase to Receiving Payments = 8 months.**

Here is what the amortization schedule looks like.

Case Study #4
Compound Period: Monthly
Nominal Annual Rate: 4.500 %
CASH FLOW DATA

	Event	Date	Amount	Number	Period	End Date
1	Loan	12/1/2016	107,456.98	1		
2	Payment	1/1/2017	544.47	360	Monthly	**12/1/2046**

AMORTIZATION SCHEDULE - Normal Amortization

	Date	Payment	Interest	Principal	Balance
Loan	12/1/2016				107,456.98
2016 Totals		0	0	0	
1	1/1/2017	$ 544.47	$ 402.96	$ 141.51	$ 107,315.47
2	2/1/2017	$ 544.47	$ 402.43	$ 142.04	$ 107,173.43
3	3/1/2017	$ 544.47	$ 401.90	$ 142.57	$ 107,030.86
4	4/1/2017	$ 544.47	$ 401.37	$ 143.10	$ 106,887.76
5	5/1/2017	$ 544.47	$ 400.83	$ 143.64	$ 106,744.12
6	6/1/2017	$ 544.47	$ 400.29	$ 144.18	$ 106,599.94
7	7/1/2017	$ 544.47	$ 399.75	$ 144.72	$ 106,455.22
8	8/1/2017	$ 544.47	$ 399.21	$ 145.26	$ 106,309.96
9	9/1/2017	$ 544.47	$ 398.66	$ 145.81	$ 106,164.15
10	10/1/2017	$ 544.47	$ 398.12	$ 146.35	$ 106,017.80
11	11/1/2017	$ 544.47	$ 397.57	$ 146.90	$ 105,870.90
12	12/1/2017	$ 544.47	$ 397.02	$ 147.45	$ 105,723.45
2017 Totals		**$ 6,533.64**	**$ 4,800.11**	**$ 1,733.53**	

360	12/1/2046	$ 544.47	$ 3.12	$ 541.35	$ -
2046 Totals		$ 6,533.64	$ 157.57	$ 6,376.07	
Grand Totals		**$ 196,009.20**	**$ 88,552.22**	**$ 107,456.98**	

Sell the Note: Now that the loan is performing, we can sell on the open market to investors for around **$52,931 today.**

Case Study #5
Performing 2nd Position Lien, FL

- Performing 2nd Lien.
- Property FMV: $210,000.
- Senior Lien Amount: $110,000.
- Senior Lien Status: Current, paid as agreed.

We purchased the 2nd lien with the intention of putting our money to work at above average rates of return. This was a buy and hold play. Collect the payments and forget about the loan. Our original yield was at 16%

- 2nd Lien UPB: $26,812
- Our Purchase Price: $11,300
- Our Expenses: $0
- Our Total Investment: $11,300

The Results: Loan is fixed rate, 30-year term. Payments of $156.49 per month. Plenty of protecting equity. Borrower contacted us 60 days after we purchased the note, wanted to pay us off. We negotiated a discounted payoff of $20,000.

- **ROI: 56.50%**
- **Annualized Yield: (not applicable)**
- **Annual Cash-Flow: (not applicable)**
- **Time from Purchase to Payoff = 2 months.**

Case Study #6
Non-Performing 2nd Position Lien, TX

- Non-Performing 2nd Lien.
- Property FMV: $376,352.
- Senior Lien Amount: $207,450.
- Senior Lien Status: Current, paid as agreed.

We purchased the 2nd lien with the intention of modifying the loan for the borrower. There was equity in the property and we had multiple exit strategies for this deal.

- 2nd Lien UPB: $32,556
- Our Purchase Price: $14,000
- Our Expenses: $3,000
- Our Total Investment: $17,000

The Results: Contacted borrower, willing to do a loan modification. Gave us $10,000 down payment to begin. Loan modified at 7% for 20-year term. Borrower pays us $252.41 per month.

- **ROI: 43.26%**
- **Annualized Yield: 48%**
- **Annual Cash-Flow: $3,028.56**
- **Time from Purchase to Receiving Payments = 12 months.**

Here is what the amortization schedule looks like.

Case Study #6						
Compound Period: Monthly						
Nominal Annual Rate: 7.000 %						
CASH FLOW DATA						
	Event	**Date**	**Amount**	**Number**	**Period**	**End Date**
1	Loan	12/12/2016	32,556.00	1		
2	Payment	1/12/2017	252.41	240	Monthly	**12/12/2036**

AMORTIZATION SCHEDULE - Normal Amortization

	Date	Payment	Interest	Principal	Balance
Loan	12/12/2016				32,556.00
2016 Totals		0	0	0	
1	1/12/2017	$ 252.41	$ 189.91	$ 62.50	$ 32,493.50
2	2/12/2017	$ 252.41	$ 189.55	$ 62.86	$ 32,430.64
3	3/12/2017	$ 252.41	$ 189.18	$ 63.23	$ 32,367.41
4	4/12/2017	$ 252.41	$ 188.81	$ 63.60	$ 32,303.81
5	5/12/2017	$ 252.41	$ 188.44	$ 63.97	$ 32,239.84
6	6/12/2017	$ 252.41	$ 188.07	$ 64.34	$ 32,175.50
7	7/12/2017	$ 252.41	$ 187.69	$ 64.72	$ 32,110.78
8	8/12/2017	$ 252.41	$ 187.31	$ 65.10	$ 32,045.68
9	9/12/2017	$ 252.41	$ 186.93	$ 65.48	$ 31,980.20
10	10/12/2017	$ 252.41	$ 186.55	$ 65.86	$ 31,914.34
11	11/12/2017	$ 252.41	$ 186.17	$ 66.24	$ 31,848.10
12	12/12/2017	$ 252.41	$ 185.78	$ 66.63	$ 31,781.47
2017 Totals		**$ 3,028.92**	**$ 2,254.39**	**$ 774.53**	

240	12/12/2036	$ 252.41	$ 3.26	$ 249.15	0
2036 Totals		$ 3,028.92	$ 113.47	$ 2,915.45	
Grand Totals		**$ 60,578.40**	**$ 28,022.40**	**$ 32,556.00**	

Sell the Note: Now that the loan is performing, we can sell on the open market to investors for around **$22,921 today.**

Case Study #7
Non-Performing 2nd Position Lien, CA

- Non-Performing 2nd Lien.
- Property FMV: $180,000.
- Senior Lien Amount: $221,000.
- Senior Lien Status: Current, paid as agreed.

We purchased the 2nd lien with the intention of modifying the loan for the borrower. This loan however, turned out a little different than expected.

- 2nd Lien UPB: $36,559
- Our Purchase Price: $3,900
- Our Expenses: $2,787
- Our Total Investment: $6,687

The Results: Contacted borrower, they were uncooperative. The couple wanted to move and leave the home. They discontinued paying the 1st mortgage shortly after we purchased the 2nd lien. Borrower attempted short-sale with the 1st lien holder which was unsuccessful. At this point we ran a cost benefit analysis and decided to write this loan off as a loss for tax purposes.

Although we have a variety of exit strategies when a borrower is uncooperative, not all deals are winners. Not all deals require borrowers to be cooperative, although it does help. In this case, we decided to take a tax loss and write off the debt.

- **ROI: 0%**
- **Annualized Yield: 0%**
- **Annual Cash-Flow: $0**
- **Our total loss = $6,687**

For non-performing loans, where the borrower is uncooperative or does not wish to re-instate (begin repaying) their loan, we have a variety of alternatives for profit. As mentioned previously we can:

- payment plan (forbearance)
- loan modification
- discounted payoff
- sales assistance (sell the home)
- short sale
- foreclosure
- deed in lieu of foreclosure
- foreclose, then rent the property (this one seems odd, although it's very profitable)

Case Study #8
Non-Performing 2nd Position Lien, CA

- Non-Performing 2nd Lien.
- Property FMV: $344,000.
- Senior Lien Amount: $321,000.
- Senior Lien Status: Current, paid as agreed.

We purchased the 2nd lien with the intention of modifying the loan for the borrower. We had multiple exit strategies for this deal.

- 2nd Lien UPB: $89,286
- Our Purchase Price: $8,200
- Our Expenses: $500
- Our Total Investment: $8,700

The Results: Contacted borrower, they were willing to do a loan modification. Gave us $600 down payment to begin. Loan modified at 3.6% for 30-year term. Forgave over $50,000 arrears. Borrower pays us $405.93 per month on $89,000 balance.

- **ROI: 55.97%**
- **Annualized Yield: 60%**
- **Annual Cash-Flow: $4,870.20**
- **Time from Purchase to Receiving Payments = 3 months.**

Here is what the amortization schedule looks like.

Case Study #8						
Compound Period: Monthly						
Nominal Annual Rate: 3.600 %						
CASH FLOW DATA						
	Event	Date	Amount	Number	Period	End Date
1	Loan	12/12/2016	$ 89,286.00	1		
2	Payment	1/12/2017	$ 405.93	360	Monthly	**12/12/2046**
AMORTIZATION SCHEDULE - Normal Amortization						
	Date	Payment	Interest	Principal	Balance	
Loan	12/12/2016				$ 89,286.00	
2016 Totals		0	0	0		
1	1/12/2017	$ 405.93	$ 267.86	$ 138.07	$ 89,147.93	
2	2/12/2017	$ 405.93	$ 267.44	$ 138.49	$ 89,009.44	
3	3/12/2017	$ 405.93	$ 267.03	$ 138.90	$ 88,870.54	
4	4/12/2017	$ 405.93	$ 266.61	$ 139.32	$ 88,731.22	
5	5/12/2017	$ 405.93	$ 266.19	$ 139.74	$ 88,591.48	
6	6/12/2017	$ 405.93	$ 265.77	$ 140.16	$ 88,451.32	
7	7/12/2017	$ 405.93	$ 265.35	$ 140.58	$ 88,310.74	
8	8/12/2017	$ 405.93	$ 264.93	$ 141.00	$ 88,169.74	
9	9/12/2017	$ 405.93	$ 264.51	$ 141.42	$ 88,028.32	
10	10/12/2017	$ 405.93	$ 264.08	$ 141.85	$ 87,886.47	
11	11/12/2017	$ 405.93	$ 263.66	$ 142.27	$ 87,744.20	
12	12/12/2017	$ 405.93	$ 263.23	$ 142.70	$ 87,601.50	
2017 Totals		**$ 4,871.16**	**$ 3,186.66**	**$ 1,684.50**		

360	12/12/2046	$ 405.93	1.82-	$ 407.75	0
2046 Totals		$ 4,871.16	$ 90.73	$ 4,780.43	
Grand Totals		**$ 146,134.80**	**$ 56,848.80**	**$ 89,286.00**	

Sell the Note: Now that the loan is performing, we can sell on the open market to investors for around **$39,456 today.**

The Business Model – General Investment Overview

You can see many of these loans were at one time non-performing. Our company model focuses on purchase, management and disposition of non-performing loans (both 1st and 2nd liens). We usually modify the loans terms for the borrower. If the borrower is unable or unwilling to work a reasonable solution, we then foreclose, rent or sell the property for a profit.

We also purchase performing loans. We buy these at under market prices, ensuring above average returns. All loans are secured by valid enforceable liens on the subject property. Most are single family homes.

During the purchase process, extensive due diligence is performed on each asset. This includes items such as title and TLO reports, background checks on the borrower, property history, and loan history. Spending extra time and effort analyzing these items gives us superior portfolio results long-term.

This business has many moving parts. It is highly profitable but requires skill and a significant learning curve. We have had success through being cautious in purchases and buying based on *value*.

How to Reach Me

Joshua N. Andrews
Notable Capital Management, LLC
www.notablefund.com
josh@notablefund.com
Office: 512-572-6900

RESOURCES

RECOMMENDED READING: MIND-SET AND FOUNDATIONAL CONCEPTS

Books to Read:

- *Invest in Debt,* by Jimmy Napier
- *The Richest Man in Babylon,* by George S. Clason
- *Taking the Mystery Out of Money,* by Lonnie Scruggs
- *The Banker's Code: The Most Powerful Wealth-Building Strategies Finally Revealed,* by George Antone

Servicing and Compliance:

- http://www.trustfci.com
- http://madisonmanagement.net

Title Services:

- https://www.protitleusa.com
- http://www.abstraxllc.com

Bankruptcy Research:

- https://www.pacer.gov
- http://www.nolo.com/legal-encyclopedia/bankruptcy
- http://www.uscourts.gov/services-forms/bankruptcy/bankruptcy-basics/chapter-7-bankruptcy-basics

Conferences and Trade Shows:

- http://papersourceseminars.com
- http://noteexpo.com

Online Discussion and Networking:

- https://www.biggerpockets.com/forums/70-tax-liens-notes-paper-cash-flows-discussion

Made in the USA
Middletown, DE
17 May 2020